WINNING AT

Acknowledgements

I would like to thank the Broadway gang – Guy, Chris, Peter, Mike, Kristian, Sheridan, Bill, and others – you got me started.

I would like to thank many poker players, writers, and industry people – Lou Krieger, Nolan Dalla, J. P. Massar, Robert Copps, Lee Jones, Linda Johnson, Mike Caro, Dave Taylor, and others – you made me grow. All of you influenced me more than you will know.

Ralph Mair, my friend and fellow amateur poker enthusiast, deserves special thanks for countless hours of poker discussions over lunch and during long road trips. Many of the poker ideas in my head are probably actually his. My great wish is to bust Ralph out in second place at the World Series of Poker Championship.

And my wife Heather. Despite never gambling a nickel in her life, she understands what a passion I have for poker. She has listened to more than her share of bad beat stories and has learned to "oh" and "ah" at precisely the right moment, even though she has no idea what I am talking about.

Illustrations by Murray Lindsay

Published by

CHARTWELL BOOKS, INC.
A Division of **BOOK SALES, INC.**
114 Northfield Avenue
Edison, New Jersey 08837

First published by Arcturus Publishing Limited

This edition printed in 2005

ISBN 0-7858-1786-7

Printed in India

WINNING AT

POKER

essential hints & tips

Dave Scharf

CHARTWELL
BOOKS, INC.

Contents

FOREWORD

I was pleased for any number of reasons when Dave Scharf asked me to write an introduction to his book. Dave is a friend of long standing. We met at the poker table, and I quickly discovered him to be a guy of many talents, and poker is only one of them.

He's a terrific poker player, but he's equally skilled as a communicator. He's far too modest to tell you this himself, but he hosts a radio program way up there in the true North, in a place called Saskatoon, where someone like me, who lives in Palm Springs, is terrified to ever venture. Most of you will probably never have the privilege of rising in the dark of a cold, wintry Saskatchewan morning to listen to Dave on the radio, but fortunately for all of us, and particularly for those of us who are aspiring poker players, Dave writes as well as he speaks – which is very well indeed.

He also has a unique gift of being able to break down complex issues into easily digested, bite-sized parts, and explain them all in a way that's easily understood. That speeds learning along. Believe me, if you're a poker player who's never thought much about the game, and have always seen it as sort of a gamble – a lark, as it were, to be played with the guys (and the gals too) for pennies, pounds, or megadollars – you owe it to yourself to give this book a read.

You're bound to learn something about poker you didn't know before. And that's a good thing. In poker, as in life, knowledge is power. And when we know something about our opponents that they neither know about themselves or about us, it only means one thing: We figure to win more of their money at the poker table.

How can I make this outlandish promise? How can I guarantee that you, dear reader, will improve your poker by reading this book? That's easy. After all, I've written five books about poker and I learned a few things from reading Dave Scharf. And if I can learn a thing or two after having scribbled more than 1,200 pages in five books about poker, I'm sure you can too.

This book is not only informative; it's a good and easy read. Dave writes in a very clear, crisp style. He is lucid, direct, and always spot-on. It's a quality we used to call "literate" during my college days, but it's found far too infrequently now.

I promise that you will enjoy this book, learn from it, and close the back cover knowing significantly more about the game of poker than you did before you picked it up – and all for the price of a few, measly bets at the poker table.

If you want to improve your poker game, pick up this book and read it; then go forth and win. That's what I've done. I hope you do too.

Lou Krieger
Palm Springs, California
June 2003

ABOUT THE AUTHOR

Dave Scharf is an amateur poker player from western Canada. He has played poker profitably for at least five years – probably longer. His accurate records extend back to January 1998. Dave has had consistent success at all forms of poker up to the $30–60 limit. Moreover, he has had a great deal of success at tournament poker, including his title as 2002 Casino Regina Canadian Poker Champion. He has played in just two World Series of Poker tournaments and finished in the money both times (5th place in $1500 Seven Card Stud Eight-Or-Better, 1998, and 27th place in $2000 No-limit Hold 'em, 2001). From September 1997 to March 1998 Dave published *Canadian Poker Monthly*, a sixteen page glossy poker magazine distributed throughout Canada and the northern United States. Dave is married to Heather and has two sons, Arthur and Oliver.

Above: The author pictured with the 2002 Casino Regina Canadian Poker Championship final table dealer, Vivianna Floer.
Also pictured (again with Vivianna) accepting congratulations, a championship ring, and $26,873 from Casino Regina's Poker Manager Stacy Delwo.

CHAPTER ONE

INTRODUCTION

Why You Bought This Book

If you are reading this, chances are you already understand that you can make money playing poker. You likely already understand that poker is a game of skill with an *element* of chance. In the short run, luck conquers all. Over the course of a single hand or evening, the *luckiest* player will prevail. He or she will win the money and the greatest, most skilled players in the world will be left shaking their heads. But in the long run... Ah, there is the rub. In the long run, skill will rule the day. Skill will prevail and the players that depend on luck alone will be no better off than if they had played roulette. Chances are, you already know this and you want to learn how to be one of the skilled players..

This, presumably, is why you bought this book. To you, poker looks like a simple and profitable game. Perhaps you play every Thursday night with a group of friends and you have noticed that one or two of your group go home winners more often than not. "There must be something to that," you think. Some are winners and some are losers and you want to count yourself among the former group. Perhaps you have been "wowed" by a major poker tournament on television and have seen players vying for hundreds of thousands of dollars. "I should learn to do that," you think, "then I would not have to work at this horrible job and I could earn a living simply by *playing cards*." Thus, you bought this book. At one extreme, you are hoping for a hobby that puts a little extra money in your pocket. At the other extreme, you are hoping to quit your job, play cards, and live a life of leisure. Will I be able to teach you to do that? The answer, like a lot of answers to poker questions, is: "it depends".

First, get over any infatuation you may have with professional poker players. You need not aspire to be a professional in order to be a great player. It is OK to be an amateur. In 1999, Irish businessman Noel Furlong won the World Series of Poker main event which is generally regarded as the world championship. He is a hell of a poker player, but strictly speaking, he is an amateur. In short, do not be intimidated, nor overly impressed by anyone who is a pro. All that being a professional means is that he or she chooses to make poker their vocation. An amateur chooses to make it his or her hobby. In fact, I know a lot of profitable amateur poker players who have rich, interesting and varied lives. I also know a lot of professional poker players who, despite making their living from a game, do not boast a lifestyle that many would envy.

Second, I have something to offer you. I remember very clearly what it was like starting out. In fact, I have been recently re-treading those steps because I have been teaching my brother-in-law Paul to play poker. We all start out as amateurs. I am closer to you than a seasoned pro who is playing year round on the tournament circuit. I have a good grasp on the questions you are going to ask.

My brother-in-law Paul is a few years younger than I am. He is a bright, single young man who has just finished a university degree in engineering. In short, he has the world by the tail. He is full of dreams and ambitions and has not yet been trapped by the obligations that come with family, children, mortgage and consumer debt. I was surprised when, a week after finishing college, Paul came to me with a request:

"Dave, I want you to teach me to become a professional poker player."

I was stunned. "What about your career? What about your education? What will your mother say?"

"Dave, I don't want to work for the man for forty hours a week in a cubicle when I could be making a living playing cards."

"Wait a second," I said, "It's not quite that easy..."

Consider the game of poker. Without a full description of how poker is played (which will be coming shortly), consider how simple the game appears to be. Each time the action reaches you, you face a very small number of options. If there has been a bet, you can either fold, call, or raise. If there has not been a bet, you can check or bet. That is it. That is all there is to choose from. Five choices and five choices only, and in the worst case scenario, you will face only three of those options. Seems simple. Poker seems even more simple if you compare it to chess.

In chess when it is your turn, you are faced with a myriad of choices. You start with eight pawns, a king, a queen, two bishops, two knights, and two rooks – sixteen pieces. The chess board features sixty-four squares. No two pieces move the same way. In special circumstances, like castling and *en passant*, pieces may move differently than usual. Chess is, obviously, extremely complex. It is because of this complexity that chess remains interesting.

Remember there is *no* random element in chess. Even after more than a century of intense study, chess remains a game in which the skilled players rise to the top and the less skilled players are left behind. After a great deal of scrutiny, there is still a great deal about chess which is not known. The *number* of choices facing each player is so large that despite years of study, some players are still better than others. Chess is so complex that you can only become an expert if you possess the right psychological aptitude and intense drive. You must study, practice, and repeat. After all of that, you still will not have played through all the possibilities, leaving open the option for a more skilled player to perform a more thorough analysis of his options and beat you.

You would *never* expect to become a world class chess player after reading a single book. Poker, unfortunately, is the same. This book will not make you a world class poker player. I am sorry if that disappoints you. This book will teach you how to *teach yourself* to become a *profitable* poker player. Provided, of course, that you make an effort to learn and embrace the concepts herein. If you want to play poker – in particular Texas Hold 'em (hold 'em) or Seven Card Stud (7-stud) – at low-limits against little-skilled opponents this book *will* teach you to do that.

If you hope to win the $2,500,000 first prize at the World Series of Poker Championship, this book will only get you started. I do not pretend that I can make you into a world class poker player because I cannot. All that I can do is teach you the fundamentals. You will have to do the rest. You will have to study, practice, and repeat.

I intend to teach you the fundamental skills you will need to beat low-limit hold 'em and 7-stud as they are played in casinos and card rooms throughout the world. Along the way I will *introduce* you to many other elements of poker; things that you do not, strictly speaking, need to know to be a profitable low-limit player. I trust that you will find the journey fun. The contents are based on a variety of things: strict mathematical principles, computer simulation, and my own experience-based opinions about what is typical of low-limit hold 'em and low-limit 7-stud games.

Why Choose to Play Poker?

Poker is a rich and varied game. It is played for pennies among primary school friends. I started playing poker at age ten against the Lipscomb boys in their basement. At the other end of the scale, poker is played for hundreds of thousands, or even millions of dollars, among the world's toughest poker pros and foolish millionaires. Of course, it is also played at all limits in between.

Poker is played in college dormitories, service clubs, and basements. It is played in casinos, cardrooms, and even brothels. Players gather during lunch breaks, coffee breaks, and spring breaks. In short, poker is played everywhere there is money and cards. You will not have trouble finding a poker game if you seek one.

Why *choose* poker over another hobby or vocation? Perhaps you are like Paul and you are dreaming of playing poker for a living. You might be like me, and enjoy playing poker as a hobby. In either case, you should pause to consider *why* you play poker. You could, after all, golf or knit. You could play craps or roulette. Why choose poker?

Let us get something out of the way up front: gambling is fun. I am a bad golfer. Horrific. For some reason (hard to understand some days), I find golf fun. I like it. My wife likes to knit. I do not. That is reason enough to pursue or avoid most activities. You either like something or you don't. So it is with poker. If you like it, play it. Don't worry about why you like it, as long as you know that you do. On the other hand, there are some concrete reasons why you might *choose* poker.

To be human is to be emotional. To delight in happiness and suffer in sorrow. To laugh and cry. To applaud your fellow humankind and to be jealous of them. I like to view poker as a microcosm of life. It has ups and downs and twists that are partly within my control and partly not. The adrenaline rush of winning a big pot is hard to top. The anguish of losing a big pot to some palooka who has never played before is tough, so tough that some people are unable to control themselves. You will see the best and worst in people at a poker table. A couple of hours of poker will give you more highs and lows than most people experience in a year. Playing poker is a roller coaster of emotions compressed into a small time period: I am happy, I am sad, I am *very* sad, I am angry and I am *unbelievably elated*. All these emotions happen in a single hand. Poker is emotionally stimulating. That is why gambling has such a strong hold over some people.

If you are good at it, poker is profitable. You will make money doing it. Either as a hobby or as a living, making money is not a bad thing. I know, I know, *money can't buy happiness*. True, but I tend to agree with David Lee Roth (on-again-off-again singer with Van Halen) who said: "Money can't buy you happiness, but it can buy you a big yacht on which you can pull up right beside happiness." This makes a lot of sense to me. Money is not the key to my happiness, but happiness is easier to find if you have the bus fare.

Poker is social. I am an extrovert by nature. I enjoy meeting people and interacting with them. Typical poker games have a lot of socializing. Moreover, I cannot think of another activity where the participants offer such incredible diversity. At a typical poker game, there are eight to ten players. In the crowd there might be a lawyer, a butcher, a businessperson, a radio personality, a real estate agent, a computer analyst, a pimp, a retired soldier, a carpenter, a farmer, an accountant, a restaurateur, a student, a financial adviser, a pediatric cardiologist, and a comedian. Actually, there is a comedian in every crowd. You may delight in sharing your time with such a wide and varied group of people in a setting where you treat each other, for the most part, with respect and interest. Away from the poker table, I would be unlikely to spend time with so many people of such different age, culture, race, and interest. For me, poker is a way to meet and enjoy some of the people that I share the planet with.

Poker is as challenging as you want to make it. There is no limit to the amount of time you can spend studying and practicing poker. As noted poker writer David Sklansky has so aptly said: "If I know something more about the game than my opponent, then I will eventually win all his money." Although poker appears to be simple, it is in fact amazingly complex. Because of this complexity, poker can become a passion that you will enjoy for your entire life.

I started my gambling career as a blackjack player. I learned to count cards and made a small amount of money. Once I discovered poker, I quit blackjack because although blackjack was profitable, it was not stimulating. While out for a ten kilometer run, I cannot let my mind wander to blackjack and replay hands wondering if I should have done something differently. In blackjack, provided you have done the background study, the correct strategy is apparent. Once a hand of blackjack is over, there is not much to re-consider and learn from. Not so in poker.

My mind frequently wanders back to past hands of poker. I replay the hand in my mind. Could I have played it differently? Would the result have changed? What factors did I fail to take into account at the time? In fact, I can list the three most memorable hands of my poker career. I lost two, won one, and learned a lot about poker from each. Even though all three examples are long in the past, I still run over them in my mind mining them for further epiphanies. The point is, poker can be as intellectually challenging as you want it to be. Spend time thinking about it, reading about it, and playing it, you will constantly discover new things.

Why wouldn't everyone play? Sounds like the perfect pastime – fun, emotional, profitable, social, and stimulating. Like I said to my brother-in-law Paul: "It's not that easy..." For every benefit, there is a cost.

First off, do not tell your minister, boss, or conservative minded mother-in-law that I said "gambling is fun." Many people view gambling as destructive and ruinous. They are, of course, partly correct. I have seen people go from non-gamblers to addicted gamblers. I have seen people trash their life savings and family relations on gambling. I have seen divorce, theft, drug addiction, and suicide all related (at least in part) to gambling. I am not going to belabor this point. You did not buy this book to hear a sermon on the evils of gambling. You bought this book to get your piece of the pie. Money is critical to the game of poker. Betting it, winning it, and losing it are all fundamental parts of the game. When you mix money and humankind you get greed. From greed, you occasionally get some very unpleasant results. For both amateur and pro, the dangers associated with gambling are ever present. Understand that if you do not respect the pitfalls, you can fall in the pit. Poker is fun, but too much of a good thing can kill you.

The emotional roller coaster sometimes takes more downturns than you would like. Even the world's best players go on extended losing streaks, and when it happens to you, you will endure a horrible toll emotionally. I am aware that my mood can be significantly effected by my short-term poker results. Recently, in a local poker tournament I was eliminated when my opponent made a 989-1 draw. More on odds later, but suffice to say, losing that one hurt. I was in a bad mood for a couple of days.

Moments ago I told you that poker was profitable. Actually, if you go back and re-read the paragraph, you will recall what I actually said: "if you are good at the game" poker is profitable. For the majority of players, it is not. Casinos and card rooms take a small cut of every pot, most players are losers. Unless you are going to dedicate yourself to becoming a good player, you can look forward to a hobby that will cost you money. If you try it as a vocation, it will end in your financial ruin.

Do you want to play a nice social game of cards? Meet all those interesting people? For every fascinating person you meet, you will meet someone you are not fond of. Not only will you dislike one, two, or more of the players at your table, but you will sit beside them for hours at a time! The green felt of a poker table is a great equalizer. You will meet a lot of fascinating people that you would not otherwise encounter, but you will also be forced to spend time with people that you would otherwise cross the street to avoid. Worse, if you are a non-smoker like me, you will have to breath their putrid cigarette smoke. Yuck.

As stimulating as poker can be, it can be too consuming. When my first son was born I realized that I would not have as much time on my hands as I did before. I had to give some things up. In my case, I stopped playing soccer and golf. I had played soccer my whole life. It was hard to give up, but I wanted to keep playing poker and I didn't have time for everything. Golf was easier because I was no good at it anyway.

Principle: *Poker can be rewarding and profitable, but it can also be destructive and ruinous. It is a choice that you make. You are responsible not only to yourself, but to others for the consequences of your acts. Make the right choice.*

There are pros and cons. What you need to decide is if poker is for you, and what you want to get out of it. You have been warned.

Paul had glazed over. If I had gone on for another few minutes I am sure that he would have been asleep altogether. I stopped.

"Have you been listening?" I asked

"Yeah. Blah, blah, blah, destructive. Blah, blah, blah, all-consuming. Blah, blah blah," Paul said. "Look, I stopped paying attention after you mentioned about the yacht. Let's get on with it. When do I go pro?"

I sighed, "You're rushing things a little don't you think?"

Playing for a Living

Aside from the advantages and disadvantages of playing poker *at all*, there are pros and cons to playing poker for a living. Most new players dream about becoming a professional rounder. I have read endless debates about the merits of playing poker for a living. It is possible, but it is not easy. It takes a special person to be a successful poker pro. I am told by those in the field that for every one person who makes it, there are a hundred who fail.

You will be tempted by the apparent freedom that playing for a living offers. No boss, no hours, and no worries. To be sure, this appears very attractive. We have all dreamed of this kind of freedom. It is not, however, that simple.

To be a successful pro you will require a lot more than solid poker skills.

You will require a big bankroll. Despite being a long run game of skill, poker is still a short run game of chance. You will suffer extended losing skids. Your poker bankroll must be enough not only to withstand these losing skids, but also to pay your expenses. To play poker you need money. Run out of money, and like any entrepreneur, you get run out of business.

You will need a great deal of personal discipline. Much more, I think, than folks with traditional jobs require. Some months you will *lose* money, which for most people, is hard to handle. Other months you will make ridiculous amounts of money. Do not go on a spending spree though, you will need those profits the next time you hit an extended losing streak. You will need the discipline to manage your life day to day, when your short term income is far from certain. This is a lot of pressure.

You have to accept that poker will, at times, become a grind. Right now poker is fun. It is new and exciting. When you switch poker from "hobby" to "profession" you can make it into a grind. In essence, you turn poker into a *job*, which is the thing you were trying to avoid in the first place!

Walk before you can run. Learn to play well. Study, practice, and repeat. Build a bankroll. Test the water. Play for a month or two and see if it still looks attractive to you.

Conventions used in this Book

Poker has its own vocabulary. If you are confused by any vocabulary as you read then refer to the Glossary on page 231 for clarification. The following table defines some of the short hand that you will find herein.

Abbreviation	Example	Meaning
Ranks are abbreviated by a letter or a number.	A	"A" is ace.
	T	"T" is ten.
	J	"J" is jack.
	Q	"Q" is queen.
	K	"K" is king.
	2, 3, 4, 5, 6, 7, 8, 9	Numbers correspond to their rank.
Hands are grouped using hyphens.	A-T	An ace and a ten.
	A-K-Q-J-T	A five card straight from ace to ten.
Suits are indicated with their corresponding symbol.	A♣-A♦	Ace of clubs and ace of diamonds.
	A♥-K♥-Q♥-J♥-T♥	Royal flush in hearts.
When the specific suit is not important, but the cards are of the same suit that is indicated by an "s"	K-Qs 6-5s	King and queen suited. Six and five suited.
When the specific suits are not important, but the cards are of different suits that is indicated by an "o"	K-Qo 6-5o	King and queen offsuit. Six and five offsuit.
Hold cards in 7-stud are in brackets.	(7-7)-9	A pair of sevens face down and a nine face up.
	(9-8)-7-6-K-Q-(5)	A straight from five to nine. The nine, eight and five are face down.

CHAPTER TWO

THE RULES

In all likelihood, you already know the basic rules of poker in some form or other. Nobody has ever learned poker strictly from a book. This, therefore, will not be an exhaustive review of the rules. It will go over the basics and cover enough that, with some practice, you will feel comfortable playing in a casino or card room.

There are lots of ways to learn the rules of poker with no monetary risk. There is some excellent software available. Easier still, there are *lots* of online poker sites which offer both play-money and real-money games. You can make a quick study of the basic rules of any form of casino-style poker by signing up at an online site and playing in the play-money games. The rules are the same as real money games, but you do not risk financial loss. *Chapter 15: Other Resources*, includes a list of software and online sites. Practice at no risk and know the rules before you make your first foray into the casino.

Also note that this book primarily addresses poker *as it is played in casinos*. *Chapter 10: Home Games* discusses non-casino games. The bulk of this book, and indeed all of this section, will specifically address casino games.

Basic Rules Common to All Forms of Poker

Poker is played with a standard deck of fifty two cards. For some forms of poker, the joker (called the "bug") is left in the deck as a wild card. This book deals exclusively with hold 'em and 7-stud, neither of which use a wild card. Suits are of equal value in poker. Bridge players are confused by this. A flush in spades is no better than a flush in clubs.

Poker requires cash or chips. It is important to emphasize that: *poker is played for money*! You can play for match heads or kernels of corn, but unless players fear losing and rejoice in winning it is not really poker. You cannot expect to bluff someone when all he or she stands to lose is four un-popped kernels of corn.

Poker is not solitaire. A minimum of two players is required. The upper number of players is limited by the size of the deck. In general, hold 'em features nine or ten players and 7-stud seven or eight players. This book assumes hold 'em games have ten and 7-stud games have eight.

Poker is "one-player one-hand". It is not a team sport. Each player plays his own hand. You should never show your hand to another player at the table. It is common practice in some poker rooms for players to show their hands to their neighbors after their neighbors have folded. Do not get into this habit. Even though you intend nothing, it "appears" to violate the rule of one-player one-hand.

The word "hand" is used interchangeably to mean both the combination of cards held by one player (Bob's *hand* was three jacks), and the play of a single game from the initial deal to the awarding of the pot (that was an interesting *hand* in which Bob's three jacks beat Paul's two pair).

"And the point of the game is to the be the one who wins the most pots," Paul declared.

"Nope. The point of the game is to make consistently better decisions than the other players in the game," I replied.

"And then you will win the most pots!" Paul triumphed

"Nope."

"What is the point of playing better than the other players if you do not win the most pots?"

I smiled. "As you will come to see, the point of poker is to win the most money, *not the most pots. There's a difference."*

Step 1: **The Cards are Dealt**

Each game begins with antes or blind bets and then the cards are dealt. The game is on. The goal is not to win the most pots, but to win the most money. As the "Mad Genius of Poker" Mike Caro so clearly teaches, if poker was about winning pots you would simply call every single hand all the way to the showdown. You would win every single pot to which you were entitled. Every pot that you *could* win, you *would* win. You would also lose a *lot* of money. The goal is to win money, not pots.

Next, there is a series of betting rounds, in between which more cards are dealt. As the hand progresses through the betting rounds, the individual bets are pulled together into the "pot." A player is awarded the pot if all of his opponents fold and he or she is the only one left, or he or she has the highest ranking hand at the showdown. Take special note of the fact that there are two ways to win the pot: either your opponents fold, or you finish with the best hand.

Ranking of Poker Hands

Cards are ranked from highest to lowest: A,K,Q,J,T,9,8,7,6,5,4,3,2. Aces are unique. They are the highest card, but can be used as the lowest card to complete small straights (e.g. A-2-3-4-5). Hands are ranked in accordance with the following table:

Royal flush
Five cards in the same suit from ace to ten.
Example: A♣ K♣ Q♣ J♣ T♣

Ties: Two or more royal flushes divide the pot. Suits do not matter. Royal flushes are technically no different than straight flushes, but they are listed separately by tradition to denote their unique status as the highest possible hand.

Straight flush
Five consecutive cards of the same suit.
Example: 9♦ 8♦ 7♦ 6♦ 5♦

Ties: The highest card in the order determines the winner. A Straight Flush of 9-8-7-6-5 beats a Straight Flush of 7-6-5-4-3. Once again, suits do not matter.

Four of a kind

Four cards of the same rank plus another card. Often called "quads."

Example: 8♣ 8♥ 8♠ 8♦ K♦

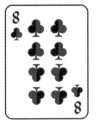   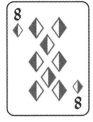 

Ties: The highest rank wins. 8-8-8-8-K beats 7-7-7-7-A.

Full house

Three cards of the same rank and a pair of the same rank. Often called a "full boat" or just simply a "boat." In Canada a full house is called a "tight."

Example: 7♣ 7♦ 7♠ T♠ T♣

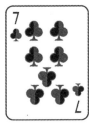    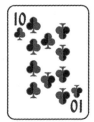

Ties: The highest ranking three of a kind determines the winner. 7-7-7-T-T beats 6-6-6-A-A.

Flush

Five cards of the same suit.

Example: Q♦ 9♦ 8♦ 6♦ 2♦

    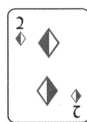

Ties: The highest ranking single card wins. Q-9-8-6-2 beats J-9-8-6-2. If the top cards are the same then the next highest card breaks the tie. Q-9-8-6-2 beats Q-9-8-5-2.

Straight

Five cards of consecutive rank (remember that aces can be high or low).
Example: J♦ T♣ 9♠ 8♦ 7♥

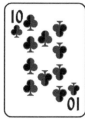   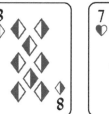 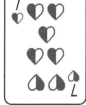

Ties: The highest card in the order determines the winner. J-T-9-8-7 beats T-9-8-7-6.

Three of a kind

Three cards of the same rank plus another two cards. Often called "trips" or a "set."
Example: 8♣ 8♦ 8♥ A♥ K♣

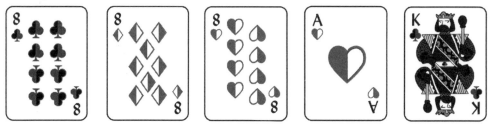

Ties: The higher ranking Three of kind wins. 8-8-8-A-K beats 7-7-7-A-K.

Two pair

Two cards of the same rank, plus two cards of another same rank, plus another card.
Example: A♥ A♦ T♦ T♠ 7♦

Ties: The highest pair wins. A-A-T-T-7 beats K-K-T-T-7. If tied the second pair determines the winner. A-A-T-T-7 beats A-A-9-9-7. If tied the single card determines the winner. A-A-T-T-7 beats A-A-T-T-6.

One pair

Two cards of the same rank plus three other cards.

Example: J♠ J♦ A♠ 9♠ 7♠

Ties: Highest pair wins. J-J-A-9-7 beats T-T-A-9-7. If tied, the highest ranking other card wins J-J-A-9-7 beats J-J-K-9-7.

High card

Five cards of different rank.

Example: A♦ J♦ 8♦ 7♦ 3♠

Ties: Highest card wins. A-J-8-7-3 beats K-J-8-7-3. If tied, then the next highest cards win. A-J-8-7-3 beats A-T-8-7-3.

If you are not familiar with poker, these hand rankings will be intimidating. Do not lose any sleep over it. Hand ranking will very quickly become second nature to you. You should, however, practice until you are completely comfortable with it. Writing them down and taking the slip of paper to the casino and referring to it as the game goes along will tend to label you as easy prey!

Step Two: **There is a Series of Betting Rounds**

Betting during a hand follows a prescribed order. One player will be designated to act first (more on this in the specific sections regarding hold 'em and 7-stud). The action moves clockwise around the table. When the action gets to you (it is your turn) you will have a few betting options. If there has not been a bet, you can either check or bet. If you check, the action passes to the next player and he or she will face the same option. If you bet, then the action passes to the next player and he or she is forced to fold, call or raise.

If the action gets to you and there *has* already been a bet, then you face three options: fold, call, or raise. If you fold, you relinquish your hand, and you no longer have any chance to win the pot. If you call, you place an amount of money equal to the bet in the pot, and the action passes to the next player. If you raise, then you not only equal the preceding bet but also increase it, usually by a pre-determined increment, and the action passes to the next player at this new amount.

Strictly speaking, you do not put money directly into the pot. You place all of your bets directly in front of you. Once the dealer has verified that all players' bets are correct, he or she will pull the money into the pot. Tossing your chips into the pot is called "splashing the pot" and it is rude. It is impossible for the dealer to verify that your wager is correct and he or she may have to stop the hand long enough to count the entire contents of the pot to ensure that is it correct.

Still awake? This may all seem complex. It is not. Find a way to practice for free – either online, with software, or with friends – and you will very quickly get the hang of it.

In a nutshell, your betting options are:

Checking: You do not place any money in the pot, but your hand is still eligible. If all the players check, the betting round ends with no additional money going into the pot. If there is a bet, then you are not allowed to check.

Folding: If there has been a bet, you may drop out of the hand by folding. You have no chance of winning the pot. You may fold any time the action reaches you, but you forfeit any money you have placed in the pot.

Betting: If there has not been a bet, you may be the first person to "open" the betting by placing an amount of chips in the pot. The other players will now have to call or raise in order to remain eligible.

Calling: If there has been a bet you put in an equal amount. You continue to have a chance of winning the pot.

Raising: A player "calls" the previous bet and raises the betting to a new level which other players, including the original better will now have to call. The second raise in a betting round is a "re-raise" and the third raise a "re-re-raise."

A betting round comes to an end when all remaining players have checked or placed equal amounts of money in the pot (all bets and raises have been called), or when all but one player have folded (the one remaining player wins the pot).

Betting moves clockwise. You act after the player on your right. Players on your left act after you. It is your responsibility to wait for your turn. Do not act out of order. Even if you know you are going to fold, do not fold early. Acting out of turn gives an advantage to players on your right who now know that they do not have to fear a raise from you. Always act in turn.

There is often a limit on the number of raises. It is usually limited to three or four, depending on what part of the world you are in. The limit on raises is usually lifted when there are only two players left in the pot. In other words, once all but two players have folded, those two players can raise and re-raise as many times as they like.

There are three basic betting structures in poker: no-limit, pot-limit, and limit. The first two are considered "big bet poker" and this book is not concerned with them.

Limit poker further divides into "fixed-limit" and "spread-limit." In fixed-limit games, all bets and raises must be the precise amount of the betting limit. If you hear someone talk about "$5-10 hold 'em" he or she is talking about a fixed-limit hold 'em game in which the first two betting rounds all bets and raises are $5 and in the second two betting rounds all bets and raises are $10. In spread-limit games, any amount between the minimum and maximum is allowed. If you hear someone talking about "$1-10 7-stud" they are talking about a spread-limit 7-stud game in which bets and raises will be a minimum of $1 and a maximum of $10. The bettor will decide what amount in between those two extremes to bet. Spread-limit is not common in casinos. This book deals with fixed-limit betting, by long and away the most popular betting format.

Poker is played according to "table stakes." At the beginning of a hand whatever money you have on the table is all that is available to you. You cannot lose more than you have in front of you, nor can you win more than you have from any one of your opponents. You cannot, at the half way

"You aren't going to teach me to play no-limit hold 'em? Doyle Brunson says that it is the Cadillac of poker games. That is the game that I want to play."

I took a deep breath. "Look Paul, you have to crawl before you walk, and walk before you run. No-limit hold 'em is the most adrenaline-pumping, wind-sucking, gut-wrenching form of poker. It is a ton of fun to play and can be wildly profitable. But you have to tune your game up in the minor leagues before you play in the majors."

"But in limit poker you cannot bet your whole life savings making it impossible for the other guy to call you because he doesn't have enough money."

"You are not allowed to do that in any form of poker. You cannot bet your opponent out of a pot," I replied.

Paul sighed, "I better stop watching old westerns on cable."

point of the hand, reach into your pocket for more money. If you run out, you are declared "all-in." You are eligible to win whatever money is in the pot up to that point (including calls from opponents who have not yet contributed the same amount to the pot). Any additional money that goes into the pot will form a "side-pot" that you will not be eligible to win.

Paul starts the hand with $10, Steve has $20, and Doyle has $1000. In the first betting round Doyle bets $10, Paul and Steve both call. Paul is now "all-in," he is eligible to win the $30 main pot. After more cards are dealt, Doyle again bets $10. Steve calls. There is now a $20 side-pot which only Doyle and Steve are eligible for. At the showdown, Doyle has one pair, Steve has two pair, and Paul has a full house. Steve receives the $20 side-pot because he beats Doyle, and Paul wins the $30 main-pot because he beats them both.

In casino poker, "cards speak." At the showdown, the highest hand that is laid face-up on the table ("tabled") wins the pot. In home games, you must often "declare your hand." If you declare a straight and you actually have a flush that is too bad for you. Not so in the casino. As long as you "table" your hand at the showdown, the dealer will sort out the winner. Even if you announce "straight" the dealer will inspect your cards and award the pot according to the actual hand ranking. You cannot err provided you *turn your cards face up at the showdown.*

The casino makes money by "raking" the pot, which means that it takes a small percentage out of each pot as profit. For example, a casino might rake 10% of the pot to a maximum of $3. As soon as the pot reaches $10 the casino pockets $1, at $20 the casino pockets $2, and at $30 the casino pockets $3. This is where it ends. If the pot reaches $1000 the casino will still only pocket $3.

Alternatively, casinos make a "time charge." All players must pay a set amount per hour to play. If a casino is "charging time" it does not take a rake.

Although this sounds complicated, it is not. You will quickly learn everything there is to learn about main-pots, side-pots, all-ins, and rakes once you start to play. Just remember this: you cannot be bet out of a hand. You are always allowed to put your last money in the pot and hope that you finish with the best hand.

Rules Specific to Hold 'em

You will find many poker variations in casinos and card rooms. Texas Hold 'em (hold 'em), Seven Card Stud (7-stud), Seven Card Stud 8-or-Better (7-stud/8), Omaha Hold 'em (omaha), and Omaha Hold 'em 8-or-Better (Omaha/8) are the most common. You will find pockets of various games by region. There is one game, however, that stands alone as the most popular the world over: Texas Hold 'em. Strictly speaking, Omaha and Omaha/8 are also "hold 'em" games, but generally Texas Hold 'em is simply called "hold 'em" and the Omaha variants are refered to as "omaha" and "omaha/8."

If you only learn one game, make it hold 'em because you will always be able to find a game. It is no good being the world's best "Crazy Banana" player if you can never find any opponents. Get to be the 1451st best hold 'em player in the world and no matter where you go there will be lots of players who are not as good as you. In fact, if you dream of being crowned "World Poker Champion," then you are going to have to learn to play hold 'em. Since 1970, the winner of the World Series of Poker Championship has been the world champion. The game is no-limit hold 'em.

It is impossible to become completely at home with the way hold 'em is played without actually *playing*. Log onto one of the many online poker sites, get some poker software, or get some helpful friends and play. You will pick it up in no time.

Hold 'em is played at a standard casino poker table pictured opposite:

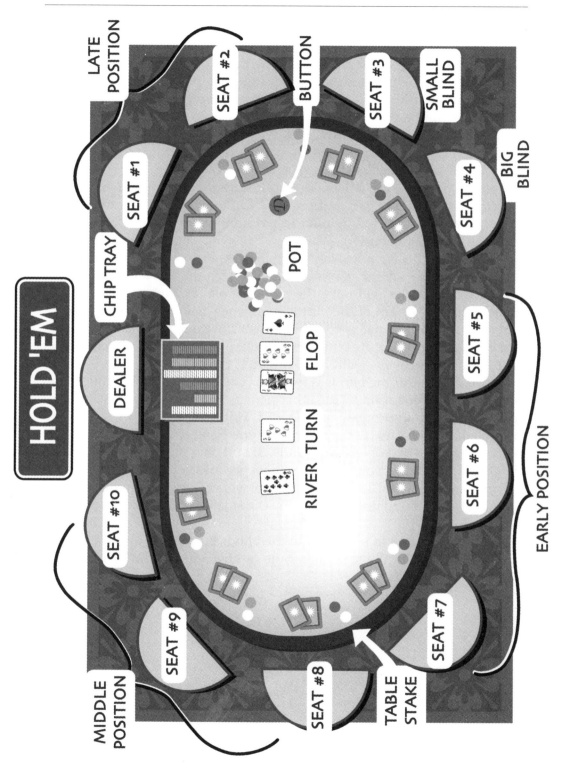

The table includes ten players and one dealer. The dealer does not receive a hand. He or she is an employee of the casino. He or she manages the game by shuffling and dealing, ensuring that players are placing the proper amount in the pot, adjudicating the showdown, and awarding the pot to the winning player. The other ten seats are occupied by the players, namely, you and your enemies.

The "button" indicates which player is the "virtual dealer." Even though the casino dealer actually deals the cards, the player with the button is said to be the dealer. The button itself is usually a plastic puck with the world "dealer" or "button" on it, but anything at all can be used. I have seen chess pieces, miniature pyramids, and crumpled pieces of paper all used as the button.

This book deals exclusively with limit hold 'em. Specifically $10-20 hold 'em will be used for all remaining examples. To start a hand of $10-20 hold 'em, the dealer will have the players post "the blinds." The player immediately to the left of the button posts the small-blind, in this case $5, and the player immediately to his left posts the big-blind, in this case $10. The blinds, simply put, are blind bets. The two players in question have bet $5 and $10 respectively, without seeing their cards.

The purpose of the blinds is twofold. The big-blind defines the action in the initial betting round – the other players will have to call $10, raise, or fold. Second, you cannot simply sit and wait until you get A-A, the best possible hand, because every ten hands you have to post the blinds. You will be dealt A-A once every 221 hands. If you only played A-A you would be $330 behind when you finally got them because you would have posted $15 in blinds 22 times! The blinds force players to play. If you do not, you will slowly be ground down by posting the small-blind and big-blind every ten hands.

With the button in position and the blinds posted, the dealer deals the cards. Starting with the small blind, he or she deals clockwise until each player has two cards.

"Listen, sorry to interrupt, but I am a little worried about what you just said. You know, all that stuff about getting aces every 221 hands. That sounds like math."

I sighed as usual. "Paul, you are an engineer, none of the math of poker is going to be hard on you."

"I knew it! I knew that this was going to turn into a math lesson! Look, I got enough math in university, if poker is all about math then I am not interested."

"Paul, I have bad news."

Paul groaned.

"The bad news is that to become a proficient poker player you are going to need some very basic math. But don't be scared away, it really is very basic."

"I see," Paul sighed.

"For instance, there are 1326 two card combinations in a deck of 52 playing cards. In other words, there are 1326 possible starting hands in hold 'em. There are six two card combinations that give you a pair of aces. A♣ - A♦, A♣- A♥, A♣- A♠, A♦- A♥, A♦- A♠, and A♥- A♠. Thus you will get aces 6 times out of the possible 1326 or once every 221 hands."

"Yawn."

"Look, it is not that important at this point. Just remember that you are going to have to play more hands than A-A or you are going to lose your money. Got it?"

"Got it."

Once each player has received both his cards, the first betting round takes place. The player to the left of the big blind is said to be "under-the-gun" and acts first. He or she must either fold, call the big-blind's bet of $10, or raise to $20.

The action proceeds clockwise until it reaches the small-blind. In hold 'em, the blinds are "live." This means that the $5 the small-blind player has posted counts towards the total that he or she owes and that he or she still has a betting option. Suppose that there have been two callers, but nobody has raised the initial big-blind bet of $10. In this case, the small blind could fold, call by putting in $5 (for a total of $10), or raise by putting in $15 (for a total of $20). Similarly, the big-blind is live. The $10 he or she has posted counts toward the total that he or she owes and he or she still has a betting option. If nobody has raised, he or she can check (he or she already has $10 in and owes nothing) or raise by adding $10 for a total of $20. The betting continues clockwise in this manner until all players have an equal amount of money in the pot or until all but one player have folded. Remember also that there is a set number of permissible raises. In a three raise game, the most that the first betting round could cost you is $40 (the initial $10 plus first raise to $20, second raise to $30, and third raise to $40). The maximum raise rule is lifted if there are only two players remaining.

Once the first betting round is complete, the dealer places three cards face-up in the center of the table (the "flop") and the second betting round takes place. This time, however, instead of beginning with the player to the left of the big-blind, the betting begins with the player to the left of the button. If the small-blind remains in the pot, he or she will be the first bettor. As in the first betting round, all bets and raises must be $10. The betting continues clockwise until all remaining players have an equal amount of money in the pot or until there is one player left.

Once the second betting round is complete, the dealer places one card face-up in the center of the table (the "turn") and the third betting round takes place. As with the second round, it begins with the first player to the left of the button. The difference, however, is that the betting doubles. For the third betting round all bets and raises must be $20. In a three raise game the third betting round could cost you $80 ($20 plus first raise to $40, second raise to $60, and third raise to $80).

The dealer then places one last card face up in the middle of the table (the "river") and the final betting round takes place. Like the third betting round, all bets and raises must be at the doubled amount of $20.

Once the fourth betting round is complete, there is the "showdown." Beginning with the player who was called, all remaining players table their hands. The dealer awards the pot to the player with the best hand. In hold 'em your hand is your highest five card poker hand made from any combination of your two hole cards and the five shared, or community, cards in the center of the table. By way of example refer to the following:

Albert: 4♦ - 4♥   Bob: A♦ - 5♦   Charlie: 3♦ - 2♥   Dave: A♠ - 4♠

Flop: 4♣ - 3♠ - 2♠ Turn: 6♠   River: 2♣

On the flop, Albert has three-of-a-kind, Bob has a straight (currently has the best hand), Charlie has two pair, and Dave has one pair.

On the turn, Albert still has three-of-a-kind, Bob still has a straight, Charlie still has two pair, and Dave has improved to a flush (currently the best hand).

On the river, Albert has a full house (the winner!), Bob has a straight, Charlie has a smaller full house, and Dave has a flush.

Your five card poker hand is the best you can make with any combination of your "hole" cards plus the five community cards. On the river the hands are as follows:

Albert: 4♦-4♥- 4♣-2♠-2♣
  The 3♠ and 6♠ are not relevant to Albert's hand.
Bob: 6♠-5♦-4♣-3♠-2♠
  The A♦ and 2♣ are not relevant to Bob's hand.
Charlie: 2♥-2♠-2♣-3♦-3♠
  The 4♣ and 6♠ are not relevant to Charlie's hand.
Dave: A♠-6♠-4♠-3♠-2♠
  The 4♣ and 2♣ are not relevant to Dave's hand.

In hold 'em, the best *possible* hand is easily determined. In the above example, on the flop the best possible hand would be a six high straight (a player holding 6-5 would have the "nuts"). On the turn and river the nuts would be a six high straight flush (a player holding the 6♠-5♠ would have the nuts).

Hold 'em Summary

Event	Description	Notes
1. Button and Blinds	Button is advanced one position, small-blind and big-blind are posted.	After each hand, the button moves one player to the left.
2. Deal	Two cards to each player.	Dealt one at a time starting with the player to the immediate left of the button.
3. First Betting Round	The "action" starts with the player to the left of the big-blind.	All bets and raises in the amount of the "small bet" of $10.
4. Flop	Three cards face up in the middle of the table.	Dealer 'burns' the top card by discarding it and then places three cards face up in middle of table.
5. Second Betting Round	The "action" starts with the player to the left of the button.	All bets and raises in the amount of the "small bet" of $10.
6. Turn	One card face up in the middle of the table.	Dealer 'burns' the top card by discarding it and then places one card face up, to the right of the flop.
7. Third Betting Round	The "action" starts with the player to the left of the button.	All bets and raises now double to the "big bet" of $20.
8. River	One card face up in the middle of the table.	Dealer 'burns' the top card by discarding it and then places one card face up, to the right of the turn.
9. Fourth Betting Round	The "action" starts with the player to the left of the button.	All bets and raises remain at the "big bet" of $20.
10. Showdown	Pot is awarded to the player holding the best poker hand.	The dealer determines the winner and awards the pot.

Rules Specific to 7-stud

Like hold 'em, it is impossible to become completely at home with 7-stud without actually *playing* it. Log onto one of the many online poker sites, get some poker software, or get some helpful friends and play 7-stud until you are comfortable with the game. You will pick it up in no time.

7-stud is played at a standard poker table:

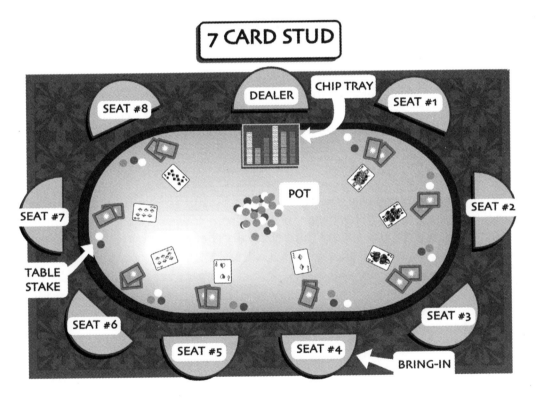

7-stud tables have eight players and a dealer. Like hold 'em, the dealer does not receive a hand. He or she is an employee of the casino. He or she manages the game by shuffling and dealing, ensuring that players are placing the proper amount in the pot, adjudicating the showdown, and awarding the pot to the winning player. The other eight seats are occupied by the players. Some locations will spread the game as seven handed and some as eight. This book assumes eight player 7-stud tables.

Unlike hold 'em, there is no button. As you shall see, the order of betting in 7-stud is determined by the players' "board" cards so there is no need for a button. This book deals with limit 7-stud. Specifically, $6-12 7-stud will be used for all examples.

To commence a hand of 7-stud the dealer collects an ante from each player. The ante is a nominal amount compared to the betting level of the game. In the case of $6-12, the ante will be $0.50. Like blinds in hold 'em, antes force the players to play. If there were no antes or bring-in bets, a player would be well advised to simply wait for (A♣ A♥) A♦, before entering the fray. Antes prevent players from pursuing such unbearably boring strategies.

The dealer deals three cards, one at a time, to each player. The first two cards are face down ("holecards") and the third card is dealt face up ("doorcard").

Once all players have their first three cards, the first betting round takes place. The player with the lowest doorcard is forced to make a "bring-in" bet. In other words, the lowest card makes a forced bet. In 7-stud the bring-in bet is usually $1/2$ the value of the small-bet. In $6-$12 7-stud the bring-in is $3. The player with the lowest door card must bet either the bring-in amount or the small-bet amount. He or she *must* make one bet or the other.

In the event of a tie, the tie is broken by suit (the only time in poker that suits are used). The order of suits from lowest to highest is clubs, diamonds, hearts, and spades (alphabetical order by the way). If one player shows the 2♦, and another player has the 2♥, as his door card, then the player showing the 2♦ will be the forced bring-in because diamonds are lower than hearts. Even in games where there is no ante (common up to $1-5 7-stud), you cannot sit and wait for (A-A)-A since you will be forced to bring-it-in from time to time.

The action moves clockwise from the bring-in bettor. Each player in turn has the option to fold, call, or raise. If the bring-in bettor has opted to make the minimum bet, the next player can call the bring-in of $3 or "complete" the bet to $6. Completing the bet does not count towards the maximum number of raises. The first betting round in three raise $6-12 7-stud can cost you $24. It could be a $3 bring-in, completed to $6, raised $6 to $12 (1st raise), raised $6 to $18 (2nd raise), and raised $6 to $24 (3rd raise). Once the bet has been completed to $6, all bets and raises are $6 despite the fact that the forced bet was only $3. You are only allowed to make the $3 bet if you are the bring-in bettor or you call the bring-in.

Once the first betting round is complete, the dealer deals each player another card face up and the second betting round takes place. Unlike the first betting round, 4th street and subsequent betting rounds are opened by the player with the highest face up poker hand. On 4th street (X-X)-A-A would be first to act. If there are no pairs showing, the best high-card hand will act first. If there is a tie, the first tied player clockwise from the house dealer will act first.

On 4th street there is no bring-in bet. The first player to act has the option to check or bet. If he or she chooses to bet it must be the amount of the small bet ($6 in a $6-12 game). Here again, however, 7-stud offers an exception. If there is an open pair showing, any player can opt to make the *big* bet ($12 in a $6-12 game). If a player shows (X-X)-A-A, he or she is first to act and his option will be to check, to bet the usual amount of $6, or to bet the doubled amount of $12. Otherwise the second betting round is like any other, betting flows clockwise around the table until all the players have either folded or equalized their contribution to the pot.

The dealer gives each remaining player another face up card – 5th street. Now each player has two hole cards and three up cards. Once again, the high hand acts first and betting flows clockwise. On 5th street all bets and raises are in the higher amount of $12; there is no option. The player who *was* the highest on 4th street may no longer hold that honor. It is possible that on 5th street, a player holding (X-X)-A-A is dealt a deuce while a player holding (X-X)-K-K gets another king. Now he or she has three kings showing and therefore acts first.

After 5th street betting is complete, 6th street is dealt. Once again the highest up hand is first to act. All bets and raises are at the higher amount of $12. After the betting on 6th street is finished, a seventh and final card is dealt *facedown* to each player (as in hold 'em this card is called the "river"). Each remaining player has two hole cards, four up cards, and a final hole card. The player with the highest up hand opens the betting in the fifth, and final, betting round.

After the final betting round there is the showdown. The players table their hands starting with the last player to be called and the dealer awards the pot to the player holding the best five-card poker hand made up from their seven cards. Think of it as discarding the two cards that are not relevant to your five-card poker hand (do not actually discard them though, let the dealer do that).

7-stud Summary

Event	Description	Notes
1. Antes are posted	Each player posts an ante.	In a $6-12 game the ante will likely be $0.50.
2. Deal	Two cards face down and one card face up to each player.	Dealt one at a time starting with the player to the immediate left of the dealer.
3. First Betting Round	The "action" starts with the smallest door card.	Suits break ties. It is a forced bet of at least the bring-in amount. Can bet the full small-bet if he wants.
4. Fourth Street	One card face up to each player.	Dealer "burns" the top card by discarding it and then gives each player one more card face up.
5. Second Betting Round	The "action" starts with the highest ranked poker hand made up exclusively of face up cards.	All bets and raises are the small-bet of $6. If there is a pair showing then a player can choose to bet or raise the higher amount of $12.
6. Fifth Street	One card face up to each player.	Dealer "burns" the top card by discarding it and then gives each player one more card face up.
7. Third Betting Round	The "action" starts with the highest ranked poker hand made up exclusively of face up cards.	All bets and raises now double to the big-bet of $12.
8. Sixth Street	One card face up to each player.	Dealer "burns" the top card by discarding it and then gives each player one more card face up.
9. Fourth Betting Round	The "action" starts with the highest ranked poker hand made up exclusively of face up cards.	All bets and raises remain at the big-bet of $12.
10. River Card	One final card face down to each player.	Dealer "burns" the top card by discarding it and then gives each player one more card face up.
11. Fifth Betting Round	The "action" starts with the highest ranked poker hand made up exclusively of face up cards.	All bets and raises remain at the big-bet of $12.
12. Showdown	Pot is awarded to the player holding the best poker hand.	The dealer will determine the winner and award the pot.

Dealers and Floor Staff

Your table will have a dealer. He or she is responsible for dealing the cards, ensuring that all bets and raises are correct, and just generally running the game. The dealer is the first person to ask if you have any questions. Did you notice a rules infraction? Maybe you think the pot is incorrect? Perhaps you have a question about something that you do not understand. Whatever the case, the dealer is your first resource. Ask him or her for help. There is no formal rule in this regard. Simply say, "Excuse me dealer, is the amount of the bet from the gentleman in the three seat correct?" The dealer will answer your question.

One level up from the dealer is the "floor person." Several dealers are supervised by one floor person. His or her job is to ensure that the room is being run efficiently. Their *big* job is to be the final adjudicator of disputes. The rule is simple: decisions of the floor are final. If there is a dispute that the dealer cannot resolve, the floor person should be called over. I recommend simply raising your hand in the air and announcing in a loud, clear voice: "Floor!" The floor person will be at the table in a moment.

Once he or she gets to the table the dealer will explain the situation to the floor person. The floor may also ask for input from the players (chances are the players will all be shouting at the floor person by this time anyway). The floor person rules on the conflict which ends the dispute. *Floor decisions are final.*

Dealers and floor people are there to run an efficient, fair game. The players are paying them (the rake). In exchange for payment, you have the right to expect efficient and fair treatment from the staff.

CHAPTER THREE

BASIC POKER STRATEGY

Basic Poker Strategy in Twelve Words

The simpler the plan, the better. Simple plans are easy to remember and easy to implement. There will be times when you will want to diverge from your simple plan. The key is, when you *decide* to diverge from your plan you must have *good reason* for doing so. The following two chapters will explain details specific to hold 'em and 7-stud. This chapter will give you basic low-limit poker strategy that you can apply anytime you find yourself in a game against little-skilled opponents.

Basic Low-Limit Poker Strategy: *Until the river, you either have the best or you have a drawing hand. Bet when you are the best, call when you have a good draw, and fold everything else. On the river, bet with the best hand and call when you have a reasonable chance of winning.*

It boils down even one step further into a simple to remember rhyme. Here is the basic low-limit poker strategy in twelve words.

Bet with the best – Good draw to invest – Fold all the rest.

Every time the action reaches you, chant the mantra. Out loud if you must, but preferably quietly inside your head. The key skill that you must develop is an excellent instinct for when you have the best hand, when you have a good draw, and when your draw is not worth pursuing. You must also learn to act outside the basic strategy plan *occasionally*, which will be discussed in *Chapter 7: Advanced Skills*. Concentrate on the basic strategy. Study, practice, and repeat. This book will not make you into a winning low-limit player. Only you can do that.

Paul studied the basic strategy for a moment. He mouthed the words a couple of times:

"Bet with the best – Good draw to invest – Fold all the rest." Finally Paul looked up, *"You want me to* always *follow that advice?"*

"Yes I do," I reassured him.

He was skeptical. "Surely the other players will soon figure out that whenever I bet I have a legitimate hand and whenever I check and call that I have a draw. They will never give me any action. They will never call. I will never make any money."

"You would think so wouldn't you? But, it just doesn't work that way in real life. Let me tell you the true story of **Cowboy Carl and the Loose Gooses.**"

Cowboy Carl and the Loose Gooses

Cowboy Carl is a real person. He plays mostly in the northern United States. Carl has what can only be described as a flamboyant sense of style. Whenever Carl plays, he wears a magnificent western shirt embroidered with two royal flushes (one above each breast pocket), a ten gallon hat (maybe twenty or thirty gallons), and snakeskin boots. In short, you cannot help but notice Cowboy Carl. He sticks out in a crowd. He is like a parade float sitting in seat three. If you were going to notice anybody, you would notice Carl.

His playing style is not nearly as flamboyant. In fact, Carl may be the tightest player you will ever see in a low-limit game. Carl limits himself in hold 'em to A-A, K-K, Q-Q, J-J, T-T, A-K, and A-Q. Carl is playing 62/1326 hands, or about one hand every two laps of the button. Assuming thirty hands an hour Carl, plays about 1.5 hands per hour (excluding his un-raised big-blind). The point is: if ever there was a super tight player that the bad players would notice, it would be Carl. It would be impossible not to notice how many hands Carl folds because it is impossible not to notice Carl.

At least, that's what you would think. But, Carl gets all kinds of action on his good hands. After two hours of folding hands, Carl is under the gun and he announces: "Raise." Five players call Carl's raise. The flop comes K-X-X of mixed suits and a betting frenzy breaks out. Carl bets out, gets raised, and Carl re-raises. So it goes until the river when Carl turns over K-K for a set of kings and wins the pot. Carl had folded almost every hand for two hours and then he suddenly went nuts betting and raising! The poor players at the table had never noticed Carl folding hand after hand. As a result, they did not know that Carl would only re-re-raise with A-A or K-K in this situation. The bad players not only gave Carl action on his good hand, they raised him several times!

Here is a player that practically has a sign above his head reading "I am a super tight player, don't give me any action." But, nobody seems to notice. If you ever ask Carl whether he is surprised that anyone ever calls him he will offer a prophetic reply, "You know, it's the same everywhere I play."

The point is a simple one. Against little-skilled low-limit opponents you do not have to be deceptive because they are *not paying attention*. Follow the basic low-limit poker strategy unless you have some very powerful reasons not to. Moreover, even if the weak players are paying attention they probably do not care what you have! They came to play cards and gamble. They are not going to throw away a hand in hold 'em like K-J offsuit just because you raised. "Any two cards can win" they will be thinking as they throw in bet after bet.

Principle: *You do not win money from good players. You win money from poor players and, by definition, poor players are not paying attention. They are unaware of how tight you are. Play the basic low-limit poker strategy against weak players.*

Basic Low-Limit Poker Strategy Revisited – Make Fewer Mistakes

Let us turn our attention away from poker for the moment and talk about tennis. Is Anna Kournikova a good tennis player? For those few not familiar with Ms Kournikova, she is a very beautiful young woman who plays regularly on the womans' professional tennis tour. Despite the fact that she has never won a WTA tour event, at present she is ranked 42nd in the world. In other words, amongst recreational tennis players she is world class, yet amongst world class players she is "run-of-the-mill."

I have only played tennis once in my life. Based upon my one outing I can tell you that I have no particular skill or aptitude for the game. Quite the contrary. I am, as far as I can make out, a *terrible* tennis player.

Now, suppose that I was to somehow arrange a tennis match: me versus Anna Kournikova. What would Ms Kournikova's game plan be? Simply put, she would be well advised to play a very basic game. Focus on the fundamentals. Return the ball into the middle of the court. Return the ball with ease. Do not attempt to charge the net or fire a blistering service ace. Do the basic things well, and do not worry about being fancy.

I, on the other hand, will guarantee my own defeat. I will swing and miss. I will hit the ball fourteen rows into the stands (I am expecting a large gallery to attend). I will drive the ball into the net. In short, I will make unforced error after unforced error. Anna need do nothing at all to *force* me to make mistakes. I will make lots of them with no help from her.

It is the same with poker. In low-limit poker you do not win money because of your own advanced skills. You win money because your opponents will make mistake after mistake. They will raise when they should call. They will fold when they should call. And, most commonly, they will call when they should fold. Nothing you do will change this phenomenon.

Principle: *Against weak opposition, nothing you do will make your opponents make more mistakes than they already make.*

Sometimes, despite themselves, your opponents will still win. For example, in a recent $10-20 hold 'em game, I raised under the gun with 8♣-8♥. Everyone folded to the button who called with T♠-9♦. *Unforced error number one.* The big-blind also called. The flop was K♠-7♦-3♥. The big-blind checked. I bet. The button called. He had two cards below the top card on the board. He had no straight draw, yet, he called. *Unforced error number two.* The big blind called. The turn was the Q♥ making the board K♠-7♦-3♥-Q♥. Now, the big-blind bet out! I folded. The button called. He had a gut shot straight draw (11-1 against making it) and he called with pot-odds of 6-1. In a moment you will learn this was *unforced error number three.*

In a single hand, this player has made three unforced errors. What clever thing can you do that will cause a player like this to play worse? Nothing. *Against weak opposition, nothing that you do will make your opponents make more mistakes than they already make.*

Incidentally, the river was a jack and after three unforced errors the bad player in question won the hand! Is that to be expected? Of course it is. Bad players will win lots of hands. As a matter of fact, I would expect that I will score a few points against Ms Kournikova in our tennis match. Chances are, one of my wild returns will land just in-bounds, out-of-reach, and I will fluke off a point. Am I going to win the match? No. Of course not. I will win the occasional point, but there is *no* way that I will win the match. The poor players will win the occasional pot, but there is *no* way that they will be winners in the long run. Bet with the best – Good draw to invest – Fold all the rest. If you can do this, you will win at low-limit poker and no deception on your part will be required.

Bet with the Best

How will you know when you have the best? To determine whether or not you have the best hand you have to take a lot into account. What are your cards? What other cards have you seen (the board in hold 'em and your opponent's cards in 7-stud)? Who are the players in the pot? What are their particular states of mind right now? Are they loose and gambling? Are they drunk? Are you drunk? What has the betting been so far in the hand? What is your position? The list could almost go on forever.

The cornerstone of determining whether or not you have the best hand is your cards, your position, and the cards you have seen. In hold 'em, the strength of your hand depends on your cards and the board. In 7-stud it is your cards plus what you have seen in the other players' hands. Practice, study, and repeat. Soon you will develop a strong intuitive sense whether or not you have the "best hand." Generally, the more opponents the better your hand will have to be. Against only one opponent, you may win with ace high. Against three or four opponents, you will usually need much more than that.

Good Draw to Invest

A drawing hand is defined as any hand that is *not* the best. In hold 'em, if I start with A-A and you start with 8-7o then I am the favorite and you are drawing. Similarly, if I start with 8-8 and you have 7-7 you are drawing. Even though you already have a pair, you are considered a drawing hand because you are not the best. You must *make your draw* to become the best. There are good draws and bad draws. A good draw will be profitable *in the long run* while a bad draw will be a losing proposition in the long run.

To sort out whether a draw is good or not, you need to understand the concepts of *pot odds* and *effective odds*. These concepts are used to determine if you should call when there are cards to come, and when there are no

"Aha!" Paul was elated. "Never draw to an inside straight. That is what my grandfather used to say."

"What was the point he was trying to make," I asked?

"He was trying to teach me that inside straight draws are bad draws and outside straight draws are good draws."

"Yes," I nodded, "he probably was. Was he right?"

"He was my grandfather. Of course he was right."

cards left to come. In other words, pot odds and effective odds are used to determine if it is profitable to attempt to improve your hand which is not yet the best (cards still to come), and to determine if you should call the final betting round just before the showdown (no cards to come). For a thorough understanding it is essential that you see David Sklansky's *The Theory of Poker*, listed in *Chapter 15: Other Resources* along with many other important books.

Pot Odds

Pot odds reflect the amount of money you must call compared to the amount of money in the pot. If the pot has $200 in it and your lone opponent bets $20, you are forced to call $20 for a chance to win $220 (the original $200 plus his $20 bet). In this case, you are getting pot odds of 11 to 1. If your chance of improving to a winning hand is 11-1 or better, then you should call. If it less than 11-1 you should fold.

To figure the chance of improving your hand, compare the number of unseen cards remaining in a deck of fifty two with the number of cards that will complete your hand. Suppose it is the turn in hold 'em and you have A-7. The board is 9-8-5-2. You are certain that your lone opponent has A-9. The only way for you to win the pot is to draw a six completing an inside straight draw. You calculate your chance of winning as follows. Of the 46 unseen cards (fifty-two minus two in your hand and four on the board), only four of those cards will complete your straight (any six). The odds against you making your straight are 42 to 4 or 10.5 to 1. In the example from the previous paragraph, you should call with as little as an inside straight draw.

You can also apply the concept of pot odds when there are no cards left to come. Suppose on the river you find yourself with top pair and weak kicker. The pot is $80 and your one remaining opponent bets $20 so the total is now $100. You must call $20 to win $100. You are being offered 5-1, which means you should call if you figure to win the pot one time out of six (win one for every five that you lose thus 5-1). If you win one out of six then five times you will lose your $20 for a total loss of $100. The other time you will win $100. After six hands you will be even. The second part of the lesson, of course, is knowing your opponent. Against *this* player, what is the chance that your top pair-weak kicker is the winner?

Effective Odds

When there is *more* than one card to come you have multiple chances to complete your hand. However, you must include the additional cost of added betting rounds. Sklansky gives us this example in *The Theory of Poker*:

> *Thus, if there is $100 in the pot at the moment and three more $20 betting rounds, you are getting $160-to-$60 effective odds if both you and your opponent figure to call all bets. If you know you won't call on the end unless you make your hand, your effective odds become $160-to-$40. When you think your opponent won't call on end if your card hits, your effective odds would be reduced to something like $140-to-$40. If, on early betting rounds, these odds are greater than your chances of making your hand, you are correct to see the hand through to the end. If they are not, you should fold.*

Let me give you an example of effective odds. You have A-7, the board is 9-8-5, and your opponent has A-9. In this situation, you will win very close to 19% of the time. For sake of this example, we will make you a 4-1 dog (80% to 20%). It is $10-20 hold 'em and there are three betting rounds left: the flop, turn, and river. Your opponent will call or bet on each. If there is $45 in the pot right now, you are getting $95-$50. You are a 4-1 dog getting a little worse then 2-1 effective odds. Fold. To be a good call you need to get $200-$50. You know that your opponent will contribute $50 in the remaining betting rounds so the pot must be $150 right now for your draw to be worth it. In a $10-20 game with one raise pre-flop, seven opponents will have to see the flop to generate $150. Not common.

Examine the following table and familiarize yourself with the odds in various situations. The table is based on hold 'em. It is more difficult to create such a table for 7-stud because the number of cards remaining in the deck will vary radically according to how many opponents you have and how many of their cards you have seen.

Number of outs	Example hold 'em hand	Odds with two cards still to come	Odds with one card still to come
1	Three of a kind. Need quads.	22 to 1 against	43 to 1 against
2	One pair. Need a set.	10 to 1 against	22 to 1 against
3	One pair. Need to pair your kicker.	7 to 1 against	14 to 1 against
4	Inside straight draw. Need to complete the straight.	5 to 1 against	11 to 1 against
5	One pair. Need to improve to a set or two pair.	4 to 1 against	8 to 1 against
6	No pair with two overcards. Need one pair.	3 to 1 against	7 to 1 against
7	Inside straight draw and one over card. Need either one.	2.5 to 1 against	6 to 1 against
8	Outside straight draw. Need a straight.	2 to 1 against	5 to 1 against
9	Flush draw. Need a flush.	1.75 to 1 against	4 to 1 against
10	Inside straight draw and two overcards. Need straight or pair.	1.5 to 1 against	3.5 to 1 against
11	Straight draw with one overcard. Need straight or pair.	1.25 to 1 against	3 to 1 against
12	Flush draw with one overcard. Need flush or pair.	1.1 to 1 against	3 to 1 against
13	Straight draw with pair. Need straight, set or two pair.	1 to 1 against	2.5 to 1 against
14	Open straight draw with two overcards. Need straight or pair.	0.9 to 1 in favor	2.5 to 1 against
15	Straight draw and flush draw. Need either one.	0.8 to 1 in favor	2 to 1 against

Paul scoffed, "I am supposed to remember all of that?"

"Don't worry," I reassured him, "You don't have to remember it."

He was still skeptical, "I am not going to sit at the poker table with a book in my lap looking things up."

"Of course you aren't," I continued, "You will calculate pot odds on the spot."

Paul sighed the sigh that I was starting to anticipate, "I doubt it. Is there an easier way?"

"I suppose there is, but it's not as accurate."

Paul perked up. "Is it accurate enough?"

I nodded, "Yes it is."

There is an Easier Way

Most decisions in poker are easy. You get dealt 7-2 in hold 'em or (2-5)-J in 7-stud and you fold. You do not have to give it a second thought. You either flop a four-flush in hold 'em or have an open-ended straight draw on fourth street in 7-stud and you know you are in for the long haul. A careful analysis of pot odds is only necessary for the close decisions.

By definition, if it is a close decision you neither gain nor lose very much one way or the other. If it is a close call, even though you are being asked to call $10 or $20, you will only lose (or win) a fraction of that amount in the long run. There is no way around the fact that you will require a thorough understanding of pot odds if you are to *maximize* your winnings. You can, however, be a winning player at low-limits with only a passing understanding.

Here is a simplified procedure. If you have the best hand then "pot odds" do not apply to you, they apply to your opponents. If you have a big draw, you can continue even if the pot is small. Big draws include open ended straight draws, flush draws, and draws that have even more outs than that. For instance, if you are lucky enough to flop a straight draw and a flush draw, you have *fifteen* outs.

If you have a small draw, you can only continue if the pot is large. Small draws include one pair with one card higher than your opponent's pair, inside straight draws, and other four and five out hands.

If you have three or less outs, fold.

If you use this criterion then you will come close enough to approximating actual pot odds and effective odds. You will be profitable in low-limit games. The basic thing you *must* understand is this: the less outs you have, the larger the pot must be to proceed.

A word of warning: be careful that you are counting *actual* outs. If you have an open ended straight draw, you have eight legitimate outs. If you make the straight you win. If all you have is two overcards, however, it is not nearly as easy to know how many outs you have. If you hold A-K and the board shows T-7-2, you may think that you have six outs (any ace or any king), but you may have three or zero. Low-limit hold 'em players love to play hands like A-2s. If you are against this hand, you have only three outs (any king). You must precede with caution when counting your outs.

Suppose the board is K♠-J♦-T♥-7♥. You hold A♣-2♣. It is the turn and the action has been very heavy so far. The pot is huge. At first glance, you may think you have seven outs (any ace, any queen). Wrong! If the betting has been heavy and three or four players are still in, it is likely that one or more players has a flush draw. It is also likely that one or more players has a queen. If these two things are true, you have at best three outs (any queen other than Q♥). An ace is no good to you because if an ace hits the river, any player with a queen makes a straight. It is also likely that your three outs will only win half the pot since someone else is likely to have an ace.

Low-limit players love to call. It is their first and foremost error. They look for reasons to call. If they have any understanding of pot-odds, they count phantom outs. You must not fall prey to this temptation. You must learn to calculate carefully the number of outs you have. Do not include cards that "might be outs." With time and effort you will develop this skill. Study, practice, and repeat.

If you find that you are in doubt during a hand, proceed only when you have at least eight outs (a straight draw) and discard all others. Even this simple rule of thumb will be adequate to beat most low-limit games. Do not use "pot odds" as an excuse to call. Although many players do, you must not. Only call when you have enough actual outs to show a long-term profit.

Principle: *When you have doubts, proceed with eight outs. Fold all the rest.*

This chapter has given you the remarkably simple *Basic Low-Limit Poker Strategy*. The next two chapters give you specific game plans for hold 'em and 7-stud. Whenever you are in a quandary at the poker table, no matter the game, limit, or opponents, you should always come back to this question: "Do I have the best hand or a good draw?" Fold the rest and things will take care of themselves.

CHAPTER FOUR

BASIC LOW-LIMIT HOLD 'EM STRATEGY

Even if you figure that 7-stud is your game, it is important to read this chapter. Many of the broad concepts covered here apply as well to 7-stud as they do to hold 'em. If you skip to the 7-stud chapter you will be missing some of the important underpinnings you will need to become a winning player.

Position

Recall the mantra: *Bet with the best – good call to invest – fold all the rest.* Almost all your profit in low-limit hold 'em will come from having the best hand, betting it, and getting called by players with worse hands. You see, in low-limit hold 'em, players do not fold enough. Your job is to acquire the best hand, bet, and let them call (i.e. let them give you their money).

Look back at the diagram of the hold 'em table on page 35. The first three seats to the left of the big-blind are "early position." The next three seats are "middle position." The final two seats (the cut-off and button) are "late position." This is important. Pause for a moment and put those definitions into your head. The first three seats are early position, the next three middle position, and the final two late position. You may find it helpful to think from the opposite end: the button and one seat to the button's right are late position, the next three seats to the right are middle position, and the three seats to the right of that are early position. If you get in the habit of counting backwards from the button, you will easily be able to adapt to games with less than ten players.

Position matters a great deal in hold 'em. If you are the button you will be last to act on the flop, turn, and river. Acting last is a *significant* advantage. If you are the button, you will have this advantage throughout the hand. Acting first is a disadvantage.

The earlier you are in the betting order, the more likely a player behind you has a big hand. If you are under-the-gun (first to act after the big-blind), there are nine players to act behind you before the flop. That is nine chances for some other player to have A-A (the best possible hand). If you are the last person to act, some of your opponents will have folded (they did *not* have A-A), and others may have just called, making it less likely that they have A-A. The later you are in the betting order, the less likely someone behind you has a better hand *and* the more information you have about the quality of your opponents' hands.

Players behind you can raise and charge you an extra bet when their hand is superior to yours. For instance, if you are under-the-gun with A-A and you raise, players will have to call two bets to try and knock off your aces. If you are under the gun with A-K and you raise, a player behind you with A-A can re-raise and you are now paying *three* bets to try and beat his A-A. The long and short of it is *position matters*, especially in hold 'em.

Position also has a psychological advantage. When you raise from late position your opponents will often think you are bluffing. It is a common hold 'em tactic to attempt to steal the blinds from late position. Even little-skilled players learn to steal the blinds and correspondingly interpret late position raises as steal attempts. When you are in late position, your opponents will tend in interpret your hand as weak.

Principle: *You have an advantage over players on your right. Players on your left have an advantage over you.*

Possible Starting Hands

There are 1326 possible starting hands in hold 'em. For instance, A♣-7♥ is one possible hand. One *combination*. If you listed every single combination, you would find that there are 1326 different two card possibilities. Even though there are all these combinations, there are only 169 different starting hands because many hands are *exactly* equivalent to one another. Before the flop, A♣-7♥ is *exactly* equivalent to A♠-7♦. The shorthand "A-7o" stands for any one of twelve combinations of an ace and a seven of different suits (A♠ -7♥, A♠-7♦, A♠-7♣, A♥-7♠, A♥ -7♦, A♥-7♣, A♦ -7♠, A♦-7♥, A♦-7♣, A♣-7♠, A♣-7♥, A♣-7♦). "A-7s" stands for any one of four combinations of an ace and seven in the same suit (A♠-7♠, A♥-7♥, A♦-7♦, A♣-7♣). All you need to understand is that starting hands in hold 'em are two card combinations that are either suited or offsuit. There are 169 possibilities.

The first, and most critical decision you will make in hold 'em is whether to enter the fray at all! You will look down, discover one of the possible 169 hands, and you will decide whether to call, raise, or fold. Mostly, you will be folding.

Your Starting Hands

Noted poker writer Lou Krieger has said: "A list of starting hands is essential for the beginner, a guide for the intermediate player, and a point of departure for the expert." It is with some trepidation that I mention this, since most players will consider themselves to be intermediate or even expert players a long time before they are. If you think you are more skilled than you are, you will tend to "over-play the game." You will make too many fancy moves relative to your ability to correctly read your opponents. Play in strict accordance with the starting hand guide until you are *absolutely sure* you are a winning player at low-limits. Then, and only then, consider adding the more difficult and subtle aspects of poker to your arsenal.

When children start playing hockey in Canada, they spend a lot of the early years on the fundamentals of the game – skating and stick handling. It is the same with all sports and pastimes. You will only learn advanced skills if you have solid fundamentals. Stick to the basics initially, then add the advanced skills.

There are several books which contain starting-hands-by-position guides. The guide in this book is tighter than most. That is, it recommends fewer hands than most. It is not, therefore, the most profitable guide for the expert. It is, however, easy to remember and profitable for a new player in a low-limit hold 'em game. It is no good to have a list of starting hands if you are unable to put it into play in the heat of combat. This list attempts to balance playability and accuracy. This list is both playable and profitable in low-limit hold 'em. Look the list over, then read the discussion that follows. Remember, a list of starting hands is *essential for the beginner*.

Your Starting Hand Guide

Two or more raises	One raise	Early position no raise (1-2-3)	Middle position no raise (4-5-6)	Late position no raise (7-8)
A-Ks	A-Ko	A-Ko to A-Qo	A-Ko to A-Jo	A-Ko to A-To
A-A to K-K	A-Ks to AQs	K-Qo	K-Qo to K-Jo	K-Qo to K-To
	K-Qs	A-Ks to A-Js	Q-Jo	Q-Jo to Q-To
	A-A to J-J	K-Qs to K-Js	A-Ks to A-Ts	J-To
		Q-Js	K-Qs to K-Ts	A-Ks to A-9s
		A-A to 9-9	Q-Js to Q-Ts	K-Qs to K-9s
			J-Ts	Q-Js to Q-9s
			A-A to 7-7	J-Ts to J-9s
				T-9s
				A-A to 5-5
A/K-K -->-->-->	K/J-J -->-->-->	Q/9-9 -->-->-->	J/7-7 -->-->-->	T/5-5
(1.20%)	(3.61%)	(7.22%)	(12.04%)	(18.06%)

Looks complicated doesn't it? It is actually very simple to remember the whole table. Start in the middle of the table with the column titled "Early position." You will be playing hands where one of the following criterion are met: offsuit cards are both queen or better, suited cards both jack or better, or pairs are nine or better. If you can remember those three things, you will be able to instantly recall the rest of the table. In fact, it is even easier. Simply remember: *early position = Q and 9-9*.

If you can remember this precept, the rest will be easy. Here are the other rules:

(1) Moving one column right or left moves the rank for unpaired cards by one;

(2) Moving one column right or left moves the rank of paired cards by two; and

(3) In any column, you may go one rank lower for suited cards.

To review, the minimum rank for two unpaired cards in early position is queen and the minimum pair is 9-9 (look back at the table and make sure you understand this). You know that middle position players have an advantage over early position players. It should be obvious, therefore, that you can be slightly more liberal with your starting hand requirements in middle position. In accordance with rule one, you may adjust the rank for unpaired cards by one. Thus, the minimum rank will adjust down by one from queen to jack. In accordance with rule two, the minimum rank for paired cards adjusts down by two from nines to sevens (again look back at the table and you will see this). In accordance with rule three, you add a rank for cards that are suited so the minimum shifts from jack to ten. As long as you can remember *early position = Q and 99*, you can quickly figure out that the next column to the right will be *middle position = J and 77*. You can play any offsuit hand in which both cards are jack or better, any suited hand in which both cards are ten or better, and any pair 7-7 or better.

What happens when someone raises? Start with early position column and remember that *early position = Q and 9-9*. When a player raises, it indicates he or she has a strong hand. Intuitively, if there is already a strong hand in the pot, you will need a stronger hand than usual to enter the fray. You will want to play a little tighter than you otherwise would. You move one column to the left and adjust the minimum rank up by one and minimum pair up by two. In accordance with rule one, you adjust the minimum rank from queen to king. In accordance with rule two, you adjust the minimum pair from nines to jacks. In accordance with rule three, you add one rank for cards that are suited so the minimum moves from jack to queen. As long as you can remember *early position = Q and 9-9*, you will know that *one raise = K and J-J*.

Principle: *In early position your pocket cards must both be queens or better, jacks or better if suited, or a pair of nines or better. Adjust up or down from there according to the number of raises and your position.*

If you cannot follow the memory key, commit the list to memory in whatever way you can. There are a couple of wrinkles that need to be explained.

The "One raise" and "Two or more raises" columns are absolute. It does not matter what your position is, if there has been one raise before the action reaches you, apply the "One raise" column as your starting hand requirements. If there has been two or more raises, apply the "Two or more raises" column as your starting hand requirements. The starting hand table is not a scale you slide back and forth. It is easy to remember if you think of it this way, but as far as raises go, it does not work that way. You only slide to the right if there are no raises. If there is a raise or two, move directly to the "One raise" or "Two or more raises" column, regardless of your position.

You will note that at the bottom of each column there is a percentage. This is the percentage of hands you will play in that particular situation. Notice that there are *very* few hands you will play when there has been a raise and re-raise before it gets to you. To be precise, you will only play 1.20 percent of hands in a double raise situation. You should be very careful entering pots that have been raised, and you should be *extremely* careful entering pots that have been double raised. I consider this to be one of the most costly mistakes made by low-limit players. They call raises too often pre-flop. If you play a hand like Q-Jo when there has been a raise and a re-raise, you not only start with an inferior hand, you pay a premium for the privilege! You will be maximizing your loss.

These percentages are included in the starting hand guide for your interest and to help you understand that winning players do not play a lot of hands. In low-limit hold 'em the player who is being selective and playing fewer hands than his fellows will almost certainly show the biggest profit in the long run. Using the starting hand guide you will play approximately one hand per lap of the button. That is, one hand out of ten.

Paul was puzzled.

"I am still having trouble understanding why a hand like K-Q is all right to play in early position if you are the first one in, but is not all right if you are in late position and there has been a raise?"

"What is confusing you?" I asked.

"A raise generally means that the raiser has a better than average hand. When you have position on a player, you have an advantage over him. Why don't they offset each other?"

"A little bit they do," I nodded. "But you are going to have to trust me when I tell you that position can only do so much. If you insist on frequently starting with the worst hand, then position will not be enough to overcome those odds. You want to have position and a better hand."

"So you are asking me to trust a poker player," Paul grinned.

"Call my bluff if you don't believe me. It will cost you a lot of money to learn though."

Principle: *In low-limit poker your profit comes from acquiring the best hand and betting it. Your little skilled opponents will call with lesser hands and you will win their money.*

In low-limit hold 'em, plan "A" is to be dealt the best hand, bet it all the way to the river, get called by a lesser hand or hands the whole way, win the showdown, and then add your opponents' money to your stack. Plan "B" is to have a decent hand, see the flop cheaply, and develop the best hand. With that in mind, you can liberalize your starting hand requirements if certain strict criterion are met:

(1) If there are two or more limpers in the pot when the action reaches you, you can play any hand from the "Late position" column regardless of your actual position; and

(2) If there are two or more limpers in the pot *and* you are actually in late position, you can add several additional hands that are not in the starting hand guide.

In low-limit hold 'em, once you get two or more limpers you can assume there will be lots of players contesting the hand. It is likely that it will be a large pot. You can afford to loosen your requirements slightly hoping to flop a big hand and take down a big pot. For instance, you are in middle position and you hold T-9s. The under the gun player limps in and the player on his left limps in. You say to yourself, "Since there are two limpers I can play any hand from *late Position = T and 55*. Suited cards can go one rank lower. I have suited cards both above nine. I call!" It will likely be a large pot and you will be able to see the flop cheaply. You can loosen up on your middle position requirements slightly and deem yourself to be in late position.

If you are, in fact, in late position and there are two or more limpers, you can loosen up even more. Play everything on the original list, plus add all suited aces not already covered (A-8s, A-7s, A-6s, A-5s, A-4s, A-3s, and A-2s), all suited connectors down to 5-4 (9-8s, 8-7s, 7-6s, 6-5s, and 5-4s), and pairs down to 2-2 (4-4, 3-3 and 2-2). None of those hands are very strong. You are hoping that you will see the flop for a single bet and flop a big hand or a big draw.

The starting hand guide is a rote attempt at playing according to the basic low-limit poker strategy pre-flop. If you follow the starting hand guide you will approximate betting with the best – good draw to invest – fold all the rest. When you enter a pot, raised or not, it will be likely that you have either the best hand or a good draw. Many low-limit players routinely enter the fray with inferior hands. Follow the starting hand guide and you will protect yourself from being such a player.

Practice online, practice with software, or practice with friends. Remind yourself of Lou Krieger's admonition: "A list of starting hands is essential for the beginner." You *must* learn the chart and become a winning player before moving on.

Paul's question reflects a mistake that is *very* common among novices. New players tend to view hands as playable or not. They do not adjust their starting requirements according to position or the number of raises.

Paul studied the table for a few minutes.

"I want to play more hands than the list. I did not drive to the cardroom just to fold and fold and fold. If it is going to be a big pot then, why shouldn't I take a shot at it with all kinds of hands hoping to win a big one?"

"How big is the pot going to be?" I asked.

"I don't know. Pretty big."

"That's my point."

Paul was confused, "What point?"

"Let me tell you the story of The General *and the* Dictator. *Hopefully it will clear up the confusion..."*

The General and the Dictator

Once there was a general. He trained at the finest military schools. He was one of the finest military strategists the world had ever seen. Far away, in a distant corner of the world there lived a dictator. The dictator was cruel and arrogant. He fancied himself a great military man. Over the course of time it became clear that he was a threat to world peace. At first he was only a threat to his neighbors since his military was small and poorly trained. Eventually, however, the threat grew as he purchased modern military hardware including long range missiles.

At length, the general was instructed to band together an army and nullify the threat that the dictator posed. The general hearkened his mind back to his military academy days. He dug out his notes and read: "In modern warfare it is good practice to take an inferior force up against a large, well supplied, and well entrenched enemy and hope that an incredible act of heroism on the part of one of your soldiers will result in victory." What?!?!? Of course his notes did not say that. His notes said exactly the opposite. Prepare an army that is superior in number, equipment, training, and supplies. The general would want every advantage over the dictator before he proceeded with the battle. He would want to take a superior force up against a small, ill-prepared enemy.

This is your goal in poker. Have a bigger gun than the enemy. Take your superior force up against his small, ill-prepared one. In other words, wherever possible, *start with the best hand*. Will the general's superior army always win? Nope. Perhaps the enemy's army is better than he thought, or perhaps through some extraordinary tactic or act of heroism, the weaker army wins.

There are, of course, occasions in which an apparently hopeless situation is saved when the inferior force is victorious due to some incredible act of heroism. A lone infantryman armed only with a pocketknife, a bit of string, and his wits defeats an entire enemy battalion. Those occasions are very memorable. We reward such infantrymen with medals and decorations to celebrate their remarkable feats. There are two things to notice. It is *memorable* and it is *remarkable*, which is good for you because you are a skilled player. Since it is so memorable, you can be sure the weak players will remember those big pots and go chasing them time and time again. Since it is *remarkable*, they will not usually catch them. They will lose a lot of money to you. Routinely play inferior starting cards and you will have to depend upon an act of heroism to win the money. Depend upon heroism too often and the enemy will run you over.

On the other hand, if you knew that the dictator was only days away from launching a nuclear missile you would be forced to attack before your preparations were complete. You could not wait for your superior army to be massed on his border. You would have to take an inferior force and through cunning tactics defeat the dictator's superior army. You would not take just any inferior force though. You would not launch an offensive with a group of irregulars or reserve units. You would use your very best. Your special forces. In other words, if your force is inferior but you are made to fight then you want to give yourself as great a chance as possible under the circumstances.

Likewise in hold 'em. When there have been a couple of limpers, it is shaping up to be a big pot, and you can enter for a single bet, you may want to take a little gamble and enter the pot with an inferior hand. But, not just any inferior hand is sufficient. Your best inferior hands are suited aces, suited connectors, and small pairs. You are hoping that through cunning tactics (position and a speculative hand that can develop into a big hand) you will win a hugely decisive battle (a big pot).

This has been a very long winded way of saying "Start with the best hand, or if your hand is not the best, limit yourself to situations in which your inferior hand can get in cheaply in a big pot."

Principle: *Start with the best hand or* **selectively** *see the flop cheaply in situations that are likely to result in big pots. Your hope is to flop a big hand or a big draw.*

The question to ask yourself is, "Do I have a bigger gun than the enemy?" If the answer is "No," the question becomes, "If I decide to take my inferior force into battle, is the risk justified by the reward?"

Paul called me after a six hour session. He was not happy.

"I am going to start playing more pocket pairs and more suited cards," he said. "It seems like every second hand somebody with a pocket pair or suited cards wins the pot. Shouldn't I loosen up in these low-limit no fold'em hold 'em games?"

"Got a few minutes?" I asked. "There isn't a short answer to your question."

"There never is," he sighed.

"It is a strange phenomenon that in the best games - the most profitable games - most pots will be won by weak players playing bad cards poorly."

"I don't understand."

"Think of it as all the bad players ganging up on you," I said. "Against any one of them your hand is much better, but against their sheer force of numbers you will frequently lose with your good hands."

Paul was exasperated. "So I should start playing bad cards poorly?"

"No," I shook my head. "You should learn patience. In the short run, it will sometimes seem impossible to beat the mob, but in the long run you will win the money."

Pocket Pairs and Suited Cards

The two types of hands that new players overvalue the most are small pairs and random suited cards. Despite studying the table, committing it to memory, and promising yourself that you will play strictly "by the book," you will be tempted, in the heat of battle, by the alluring siren song of little pairs and suited cards.

Small pairs look attractive for two reasons. You already have a pair and you could win the hand without improving or you might flop a set. True and true, but unlikely. Consider the likelihood of 2♣-2♦ beating A♣-K♦. To be specific, the 2♣-2♦ will win 52.258% of the time. Sounds promising. The 2-2 is the favorite! What if a player with Q♥-T♠, is also in the hand? Now the 2♣-2♦ only wins 29.860% of the time. Let us add one more hand to the mix. What if someone has 3♥-3♠? Now the 2♣-2♦ will win only 15.851% of the time. Considering that with four players in a hand you would intuitively hope to win 25% of the time, 15.851% is very poor. It is actually even worse because the percentages just quoted are Monte Carlo simulations – all players calling all bets and raises all the way to the river. You will actually win less than 15.851% of hands with your deuces because you will frequently fold long before you hit your third deuce! Worse still, sometimes you will go all the way to the river, hit your miracle third deuce, and lose even more money because you were drawing dead all along.

In low-limit hold 'em, it is rare for a small pair to hold up on its own because there are a lot of players contesting each pot. You will have to make three of a kind to win. You do not make three of a kind very often. The key to playing small pairs successfully is to get in cheap, flop a set, and win a big pot. Fold on the flop if you miss. This is what the starting hand guidelines are *precisely* designed to do. The *only* time you should play 2♣-2♦ is when you are in late position (button or one before) *and* there have been two limpers. In this case, you can figure that there is a reasonable chance of getting to see the flop for only one bet. Further, if you do flop a set you will have at least three opponents (two limpers and the big blind) to win money from. In other words, you are likely to win a big pot.

What about suited cards? Consider an example. You hold T♣-8♣, and your opponent holds A♣-K♦. The T♣-8♣ will win 38.972% of the time. Compare this to A♣ K♦ versus the offsuit version T♣-8♠. The T♣-8♠ will win 36.007% of the time. In a heads-up matchup, being suited only adds about three percent to your chance of winning.

Just as small pairs need to make a set to win, random suited cards need to hit a big hand to win (either a flush or two pair). This does not happen very often. Like small pairs, you want to get in cheap, luck into a great flop, and win a big pot.

In low-limit hold 'em you will see pot after pot won with hands like 4-4 and J-6s. Make a note of the players winning these pots. You are only seeing their pocket cards when they win. You are not seeing their cards every time they miss their flush draw (after calling pre-flop, on the flop, and on the turn). You are not seeing their cards every time they go to the river with their 2-2 and call "just in case you are bluffing." You are not seeing their cards every time they squander their chips chasing the dream of a flush or a set. They will lose so much money in pursuit of happiness, when it finally arrives (they river their flush), the money they win will not equal all that they have lost.

Each session there will be one or two lucky players who will hit more than their share of flush draws and have great huge stacks of chips in front of them. They are depending upon heroic acts to win the day. Some days it will work, but in the long run they will lose the war (not to mention their house, car, and kid's education). Do not be tempted.

Principle: *For small pairs and suited cards to be profitable, they require getting in cheap and winning big. This opportunity does not present itself very often. Do not talk yourself into playing small pairs or suited cards in other circumstances.*

The Big-Blind and the Small-Blind

The starting hand guide says nothing of the big-blind or the small-blind. The blinds are unique for a couple of reasons. Pre-flop they are actually the last two hands to act. From a positional standpoint it is actually advantageous to be in the small-blind or big-blind *pre-flop*. This, however, is where your positional advantage ends. On the flop, turn, and river the blind players will be the first to act. You will be giving up position to every other player at the table for the next three betting rounds, including the two betting rounds in which the bet size doubles. Not only this, but the relative strength of hands becomes much more clearly defined on the flop. Do not get excited by the small advantage of acting last pre-flop. The disadvantage of acting first on the next three betting rounds is extreme.

The other unique thing about the blinds is that it will cost you less to see the flop. If there are no raises, the small-blind is half price and the big-blind is free. You get to see the flop without paying anything. You should note that I said, "It will cost you less to enter the pot." I did not say, "You already have money in the pot." You will hear this sort of phrase a lot at low-limit hold 'em tables. Another of my favorites is, "I had to defend my blind." Nonsense! You do not have to defend anything. The amount of money you personally have put into the pot has no bearing on whether or not you should put in *any more* money. You should proceed with the hand, or not. You are in a profitable situation, or not. The amount of money you have put in the pot does not matter. The *total* size of the pot does.

Principle: *Do not **ever** feel compelled to protect your blinds. The fact that you have posted a blind does not bear on whether or not you should proceed. Proceed if you have a profitable situation and fold if you do not. Wave goodbye to your blind if you must, but fold nonetheless.*

What constitutes a profitable situation? The answer, of course, is "it depends." Pre-flop think of the small-blind as late position and proceed accordingly. If there has not been a raise, you can play any of the late position hands. If there have been two limpers, you can extend your hands to include all suited aces, suited connectors down to 5-4s, and all pocket pairs. This is a large list to play in early position (remember that you are going to be first to act in all succeeding betting rounds), but you are paying half price. Remember the General and the Dictator? For half price you can be a little bit speculative and hope for a heroic victory in a big pot. If there has been one or two raises then apply the one raise or two raise columns.

If you are the big blind and there has not been a raise then check. You get to see the flop for free. If there has been a raise, it would be incorrect to play hands only from the "one raise" column, since in your case you can see the flop for half-price. In a $10-20 game where there has been one raise, other players have to call $20 but you only have to call $10. You can afford to be more liberal. In a typical low-limit game, call one raise in the big blind with any "late position" hand and call two raises with any "one raise" hand.

Principle: *Consider the small blind to be late position. In the big blind, call one raise with late position hands, call two raises with one raise hands, and call three raises with two raise hands.*

If it is Raised Behind You

Despite your best laid plans, sometimes a player behind you raises and you are not allowed to "get in cheap." It is $10-20 hold 'em. You have A-4s on the button. There are two limpers. You limp in. The small blind limps in. You lick your lips. You got in cheap and it is going to be a big pot. Then the big-blind raises! So much for getting in cheap.

The situation, however, is not all that desperate. In the example just given, assuming that all the limpers call the big blind's raise (and in low-limit hold 'em they will), the pot will be $90 by the time it gets back to you; $20 from each player plus your original $10. Call. No questions asked. Even if the big blind has A-A you are not a 9-1 dog.

The simplest approach to a raise behind you after you have limped in is to think of yourself as a big-blind. Call one raise with whatever you have. Since you entered the pot with a legitimate holding in the first place, it is legitimate to call one more bet no matter what you have. Call two raises behind you with one raise hands, and call three raises behind you with two raise hands.

Back to the example. If it is one raise back to you then call. If the big blind raised and one of the original limpers re-raised then it is two raises back to you and you must fold. You can only call two raises with one raise hands and three raises with two raise hands.

Playing Your Hand Pre-flop

So far we have talked about the hands that you will play, but not how to play them. To determine how to play a particular hand pre-flop, turn your mind back to the basic low-limit poker strategy:

Bet with the best – Good draw to invest – Fold all the rest.

Remember K-I-S-S: "Keep It Simple, Stupid." You do not have to be fancy to beat low-limit hold 'em games. All you need to do is start with quality cards, bet when you have the best hand, call when you have a good draw, and fold everything else.

Next, you need to understand how various hands stack-up against one another in order to determine when you are likely to have the best hand and when you are likely to have a good draw. Take a look at the following table. It shows hand match-ups. The table has limited use since it only shows heads-up match-ups and most pots are multi-way contests. Further, it is made up of Monte Carlo simulations. It does not simulate any betting. It is as if both players call all bets to the river and turn over their cards to see who wins. Nevertheless, it is an excellent guide as to the relative strength of hands.

Title	Example	Percentage and Odds Win	Your Edge
One pair v No pair (top duplicated)	Q♠-Q♣ v Q♥-J♦	88% v 11% 8 - 1	Huge edge
One pair v No pair (both lower than pair)	Q♠-Q♣ v J♥-T♦	85% v 15% 5.7 - 1	Huge edge
One pair v Lower pair (under pair)	Q♠-Q♣ v J♠-J♣	81% v 19% 4.0 - 1	Huge edge
Two big v No pair (top duplicated)	K♠Q♣ v Q♥-J♦	74% v 26% 3.0 - 1	Big Edge
Two big v No pair (bottom duplicated)	A♠-Q♣ v K♥-Q♦	74% v 26% 3.0 - 1	Big Edge
Two big v No pair (no over - top duplicated)	K♠-Q♣ v K♥-J♦	74% v 26% 3.0 - 1	Big Edge
One pair v No pair (one card above pair)	Q♠-Q♣ v A♥-J♦	71% v 29% 2.4 - 1	Big Edge
One pair v No pair (bottom duplicated)	Q♠-Q♣ v K♥Q♦	69% v 31% 2.2 - 1	Big Edge
No pair v No pair (both over the other)	K♠-Q♣ v J♥-T♦	64% v 36% 1.8 - 1	Small Edge
No pair v No pair (one over and one middle)	K♠-J♣ v Q♥-T♦	62% v 38% 1.6 - 1	Small Edge
No pair v No pair (one over and one under)	K♠-T♣ v Q♥-J♦	59% v 41% 1.4 - 1	Small Edge
One pair v No pair (both over pair)	2♠-2♣ v A♥-K♦	53% v 47% 1.1 - 1	Negligible Edge

No matter how big a pre-flop edge you get, your opponent still has some chance to win. Most new players do not understand how hands match up. Most new players feel that the best hand ought to win. The truth is, in most low-limit hold 'em games the best hand pre-flop is the favorite, but will probably lose. Huh? Let me explain. If you give one player A-A and run Monte Carlo simulations, you discover that A-A will beat two opponents about 73% of the time, three opponents about 64%, four opponents about 56%, and five opponents about 49% of the time. Aha! Once you get to five opponents A-A is the favorite, but it will probably lose. Does that mean you should not bet with it? No. Of course not.

If you and your five opponents each put up $10 per hand and you were dealt A-A every time, you would make a lot of money. For every one hundred hands you would win forty-nine. 49 x $50 = $2450 that you win. The other fifty-one times you lose. 51 x $10 = $510 that you lose. Even though you will probably lose you come out $1940 ahead for every one hundred hands you play. Of course, this example is distant from the way poker is actually played, but it is sufficient to illustrate the principle.

Principle: *If you have the best hand with cards yet to come then bet. Often you will find yourself in a situation in which you will probably lose, but you will come out ahead in the long run.*

By the way, things get quite a bit more drastic if your hand is not as good as A-A. In Monte Carlo simulations, A-K beats one opponent about 65% of the time, and two opponents about 48% of the time. In other words, even though a hand as powerful as A-K is the favorite, it quickly becomes a probable loser in Monte Carlo simulations. The long and short of it is this: starting with the best hand means that you have the best chance of winning (you are the favorite), but it is possible to be in a situation in which you will probably lose. Get used to it. This is poker. If the player with the least chance of winning (the dog) did not beat the favorite some of the time, nobody would play because the weak players would lose all of their money – quickly.

To get a huge edge against one opponent you must be holding a pair. Big pairs are, obviously, powerful holdings. If you hold A-A against only one opponent then you know that you have a huge edge (ignoring the possibility that he or she also has A-A which you intuitively know to be fifty-fifty). There is one way and one way only to get a huge edge... start with a big pair that matches up well against your opponent. When you peek at your pocket cards and you see A-A, K-K, Q-Q, or J-J, then get excited. You have a rare and very profitable starting hand.

To get a big edge the hands must match up such that your opponent has only three outs. Only one of his cards is available to beat you. In other words, one of his two cards will not beat you if he or she pairs it. For example, in A-Q v K-Q it does the K-Q no good to flop another Q since the A-Q has a better kicker. The K-Q needs to pair the king to win. Only one of his or her cards is "working." He or she has only three outs.

As far as I know, Roy Hashimoto coined the term "dominated hand" to refer to situations in which one hand has a *huge* or *big* edge – situations in which the dog has three or less outs pre-flop.

Small edges are any situation involving two unpaired cards versus two unpaired cards where both players have both cards working. This is a common hold 'em match up. Note also that K-Q v J-T is about the same as K-Q v 6-5. The favorite is not that huge of a favorite and the dog is not that big of a dog.

Finally, a negligible edge occurs when a pair takes on two overcards.

With all of this in mind, let us look at various starting hands and figure out how to play them pre-flop. Generally, your pre-flop holding will divide into one of seven categories: big pairs, medium pairs, small pairs, big aces, suited aces, random big cards, and small suited connectors. You know nothing about your opponents hole cards yet you want to *Bet with the best - Good draw to invest - Fold all the rest*. Simple right?

Big Pairs

Big pairs are A-A, K-K, Q-Q, and J-J. It should be obvious to you that there is a significant chance that you will dominate a lot of different hands when you hold aces, kings, queens, or jacks. For instance A-A dominates *everything*. K-K dominates *everything* other than A-A. Q-Q dominates everything other and A-A, K-K, and A-K. And, J-J dominates everything other than A-A, K-K, Q-Q, A-K, A-Q, and K-Q.

According to the *Basic Low-Limit Poker Strategy*, what should you do? Raise. In fact, you should probably re-raise with all four and cap the betting (put in the 3rd raise) with A-A and K-K. Pre-flop, there is every reason to believe you have the best hand. Your pair of kings will occasionally run into aces, but only rarely.

Principle: *With big pairs (A-A, K-K, Q-Q, and J-J) you should raise pre-flop. Cap the betting with A-A and K-K.*

Medium Pairs

Medium pairs are T-T, 9-9, and 8-8. In a heads up confrontation they do very well. 9-9 for instance will win 72.1% of the time against a random hand. Very impressive. The problem, of course, is you will not be playing against a random hand. You will be playing against a hand or hands that your opponents have *chosen* to play.

With middle pairs you *will* dominate a lot of hands that low-limit players love to play. Hands like A-5s and 4-4. On the other hand, you will often be up against hands like K-To which you are a negligible favorite over. Low-limit hold 'em players call too much. They love any two big cards. If there is a raise then you know to tighten up considerably to avoid being dominated. Your opponents do not know this. They like to be dealt K-Jo. They will play K-Jo 100% of the time. It does not matter to them if there has been a raise or not. They have a list of hands that are playable and a list of hands that are not playable and they simply follow their list. One, two, or three raises do not matter to them.

With medium pairs, raise if you think you can manipulate the situation such that you will be left with only one or two opponents. This will occur either if the game is tight and players are folding against a raise, or if you are in late position and there has been one caller or no callers. If you are in a *typical* low-limit game where raises do not cause your opponents to fold hands like K-To, then you should just call and see what the flop brings. Either you have a negligible edge against two random big cards, or you are a huge dog to a bigger pair.

Think of medium pairs as big pairs in tight games and small pairs in loose games. In a tight game, 8-8 may win without improving. In a loose game, 8-8 will probably have to make a set to win. If the game is tight, raise and hope to play your middle pair against one or two opponents. If the game is loose, call and hope to flop a set.

Principle: *Medium pairs (T-T, 9-9, and 8-8) should be played as big pairs in tight games and small pairs in loose games. Most low-limit hold 'em games are loose. In most low-limit games you will play medium pairs as though they are small pairs.*

Small Pairs

Small pairs are defined as 7-7, 6-6, 5-5, 4-4, 3-3, and 2-2. Most low-limit hold 'em players play small pairs very poorly. Most low-limit players play all pocket pairs in all situations. The dream of flopping a set and winning a huge pot is just too tempting. Do not fall into this trap!

Obviously there are very few hands that you will dominate with your small pair. What are you hoping your opponent holds? A pair smaller than yours? A-2s? What if you have several opponents? You are a negligible favorite over two bigger cards, but you are a huge dog to a bigger pair. Herein lies the problem with small pair. You are either a negligible favorite or a huge dog.

There are two ways for your small pair to win. First, all of your opponents could miss their hands and you could win without improving. Second, you could improve to a set, straight, flush, full house, quads, or a straight flush and beat a hand which would otherwise beat your pair.

What are the chances that your small pair will win the pot in a low-limit game without improving? Without knowing all of the variables, this is an impossible question to answer precisely. In particular, small pairs are interesting creatures because they are weak when played against a big field and strong when played heads up. For instance, if you suppose the board is K-J-7-3-2 and you have 4-4 (you have not improved) then you will win 57.8% of hands played heads up against two random cards. Your 4-4 exceeds the expectation of a random hand (which you intuitively know to be 50%). On the other hand, with that same board of K-J-7-3-2, your 4-4 will win only about 18% of the time against three opponents, which is below the expectation of a random hand (which you intuitively know to be 1 in 4 or 25%). The lesson is, in games where there tend to be a lot of opponents, it becomes increasingly unlikely that your hand of 4-4 will win unimproved. In fact, with the same board of K-J-7-3-2 your 4-4 will only win 0.2% of the time against nine opponents. The example is not perfect, but it does demonstrate that your small pair must improve in multi-handed pots if it is to win.

Since your pocket pair must improve to win you can assume, in accordance with the *Basic Low-Limit Poker Strategy*, that your small pair is not the best – it is a drawing hand. The question is this: under what circumstances is seeing the flop with your small pair considered to be a "good" draw?

With a pocket pair you will flop a set about 10% of the time. Not very often. If you do not flop a set you will usually be forced to fold because if there is any betting, your small pair is likely beat and you have very little chance of improving (you have only two outs). You have two things working against you: you are starting as a long shot and you will have to fold your small pair if there are over cards on the flop and any betting.

The answer is contained in the table of starting hands. You will be playing small pairs in middle or late position for a single bet, usually when there is multi-way action. You will be entering the pot at minimum cost, in situations which favor the possibility of winning a big pot. Do not raise with small pairs pre-flop. Treat them as drawing hands.

Big Aces

Big aces are defined as A-K, A-Q, and A-J, suited or not. Like big pairs, big aces will often dominate their opponents. Low-limit hold 'em players love to play any two cards ten or above. Big aces will fair very well against hands like K-J, Q-T and J-T. Frequently low-limit players will call with hands that are a long way behind. Furthermore, big aces are rarely dominated. Even if you do not dominate the opposition you are probably still ahead or, in the worst case scenario, not very far behind. Compare this to small pairs. Small pairs are either a little bit ahead or a long way behind. Not so with big aces which can be a long way ahead, a little way ahead or a little bit behind. Rarely are they a long way behind.

Go ahead and assume that your big ace is the best and raise. Remember though that if there has already been a raise you must tighen up to A-Ko, A-Ks, and A-Qs. Even with these hands, you can go ahead and put in the second raise. There is still a good chance that you will dominate your opponents.

Suited Aces

Suited aces are defined as A-Ts to A-2s. Similar to small pair, suited aces will tend to be a little bit ahead or a long way behind. Negligible favorite or huge dog. Your suited ace will be a little bit ahead of any unpaired two cards that do not contain an ace. You will even dominate an unpaired hand that matches up to your kicker. On the other hand, you are in big trouble against big aces and pocket pair bigger than your kicker.

Like small pairs and medium pairs, you will have a great deal of trouble knowing where you stand pre-flop if you are holding suited aces.

Like small pair, treat them as a drawing hand and look to get in cheap in a big pot. Pairing your ace may be enough to win but you are hoping for two pair or a flush.

Random Big Cards

Big cards are defined as any two cards, both ten or higher not yet covered: A-T, K-Q, K-J, K-T, Q-J, Q-T, and J-T. In low-limit hold 'em a lot of players will play random big cards without regard to their position or the number of raises. When you are holding random big cards, you will have to be lucky to dominate your opponents. You will have to be fortunate to have K-J when your lone opponent has K-T. Sometimes you will dominate and sometimes he or she will. You will not have any confidence in the relative strength of your hand until the showdown. In other words, for every time that K-J runs into K-T, it will run into A-K. That is, for every time that you accidentally dominate the opposition you will be dominated by them. Call before the flop. On the flop, turn, and river you will have a much better idea where you stand. This is *not* to suggest that you play any two big cards. Play them only in accordance with the starting hand guide.

Small Suited Connectors

Small suited connectors are defined as two cards of the same suit of adjacent ranks. They include T-9s, 9-8s, 8-7s, 7-6s, 6-5s, and 5-4s. Note that the cut off is 5-4s, because 4-3s has fewer ways in which to make a straight.

Like small pairs, small suited connectors are often played badly by little-skilled players. They are looking for hands to play; they are not looking for hands to fold. When the possibility of either a straight or a flush presents itself, they definitely want to see the flop. Do not fall prey to this trap. Is 5-4s the best hand? No. Then, by definition it is a drawing hand. Furthermore, it is likely to need a lot of help – two pair, a straight, or a flush. Great risk requires great reward. Small suited connectors require that you get in cheap with the prospect of a big pot.

"So what you are saying is 'raise with big pair and big aces' and call with everything else?" Paul asked.

"Yes," I answered. "That will do for now. As you get better and you learn more about your opponents you may choose to raise with more hands, particularly in late position. Meanwhile, do not get aggressive with your weaker hands. See the flop and see what it brings. If you hit your hand **then** *you are likely to be the best."*

Playing After the Flop

Choosing to play a hand or not is the most critical decision you will make in a hand of hold 'em. The flop will be the second most critical junction. On the flop you will choose to continue or not. If you go beyond the flop then you will probably go all the way to the river. Do not get into the habit, like many low-limit players, of routinely seeing the turn. On the flop, either you are the best or you have a good draw. Many players will take off the turn with a poor draw because it only costs a small bet (betting doubles on the turn). Do not get into this habit. Bet if you are the best. See the turn if you have a good draw. Fold all the rest.

What is likely to be the best hand on the flop? One pair is often enough to win. Generally, you are hoping to have "top pair" or better. That is, you would like one of your pocket cards to pair the highest card on the flop. You are said to have "top pair." A flop in which you have better than top pair is also strong – a pair bigger than the board, two pair, a set, or even better.

In hold 'em the board will go a long way towards determining the strength of hand you likely need to win. What follows is a look at each category of hand and suggestions about the kinds of flop that you are looking for. This is by no means an exhaustive list. It is a starting point. There is no substitute for "study, practice, and repeat."

Big Pairs

A single pair is often enough to win in hold 'em. Herein lies the power of the big pocket pair. You already have a pair. Your opponents are trying to outdraw you. With any of A-A, K-K, Q-Q, or J-J you are hoping to flop three cards below your pair. Most profit in low-limit hold 'em comes from acquiring the best hand, betting, and letting your opponents call. An ideal situation arises when you hold a hand like K-K, the flop is Q-T-2, and you are against a couple of opponents, one who holds A-Q and the other K-T. In this situation you are better than a 2 - 1 against the field; you are better than 2 -1 to beat both opponents.

Green light flops

You should be very aggressive with green light flops. You probably have the best hand and your opponents are probably drawing thin. For each of the following examples, assume that you have two kings.

Your hand:

The flop:

You have flopped quads. The only way for your opponents to beat you is to draw two perfect cards (turn and river) to make a straight flush which is, of course, extremely unlikely. You are virtually unbeatable. You can be as aggressive as you like.

The flop:

You have flopped top set. You have the nuts. You are not, of course, guaranteed victory. If one of your opponents has Q-J then he or she holds an open straight draw. He or she will win a little better than 25% of the time. On the other hand, if you are against a lone opponent who holds K-Q, he or she will only win 3% of the time. When you have a strong hand do not be afraid of your opponents' draws. Make them pay to get there. Most of the time they will not and you will win their money.

The flop:

You have flopped an overpair. This is the most common green light flop for your big pair. It is a very profitable situation. An opponent with A-Q is drawing thin but will give you lots of action. You should be aggressive.

Amber light flops

When you get an amber light flop you can test the water. You may have the best hand, but it is more difficult to know. You can bet, but if the betting gets heavy you need to have some very compelling reasons to continue. For each of the following examples, assume you have two kings:

Your hand:

The flop:

You have an overpair, but the flop is coordinated. Coordinated flops are dangerous because they give your opponents lots of possibilities. Low-limit hold 'em players frequently overvalue suited connectors and random suited cards. One of your opponents may already have made two pair. If not, there may be a flush or a straight draw against you. Maybe both. Against a coordinated flop you are probably still the best, but beware if heavy betting breaks out. If the turn card is a scary card like a 5 you should have no shame in folding. In fact, knowing when to fold top pair and overpair is a critical skill.

The flop:

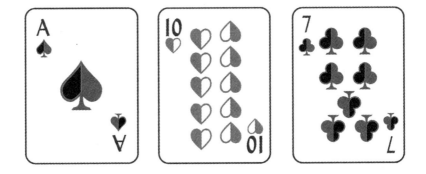

When there is an overcard to your big pair you need to consider whether or not one of your opponents has paired the overcard. If he or she has, then you find yourself with only two outs. The more opponents you have, the more likely it is that someone has paired the top card on board. There is an additional likelihood of one of your opponents pairing the overcard when it is an ace because low-limit players love aces, particularly suited aces. If you have one or two opponents when one overcard flops, you can bet. If you are raised, or if one of your opponents bets into you, generally you should fold. This is a tricky area and you will have to learn, with experience, when your big pair is likely to be the best despite the presence of one overcard. Proceed with extreme caution. When in doubt, fold. Low-limit players lose a lot of money by refusing to fold big pairs when they are beat.

The flop:

Paired boards are dangerous because if one of your opponents has made trips you are drawing very thin. You have only two outs. Paired boards are particularly dangerous if it is a high pair since the likelihood of one of your opponents playing a high card is greater than a low card. Compare a flop of Q-Q-7 to a flop of Q-7-7. It is more likely that one of your opponents has a queen than a seven. Queens are high cards and your low-limit opponents love high cards. Proceed with caution.

A Final Word About Big Pairs

Big pairs are hugely profitable, but a lot of low-limit players refuse to ever fold them. They wait all night to get K-K and when they finally do, they refuse to fold even with an ace on board and heavy betting. Remember, *there is no shame in folding.* Maximizing your wins is important, but minimizing your losses is just as important. Starting with a strong hand does not mean you will finish with one. When you are beat and you do not have a good draw then fold. Simple as that. Do not fall in love with your big pairs. Like any hand, they are only profitable if you play them well.

Medium Pairs

A single pair is often enough to win in hold 'em, but it needs to be a large pair compared to the board. In other words, the more overcards to your pair that are on the board, the more likely that your pair is no good. The smaller your pair the more likely that there will be overcards. There is an additional danger with medium pairs T-T, 9-9, and 8-8. When you flop an overpair to the board, the board will be bunched. If your 8-8 is an overpair to the board, all five of the board cards will be between seven and deuce. The board will be coordinated and overpairs do not fair as well against coordinated boards.

Green light flops

For each of the following examples, assume you have a pair of nines:

Your hand:

The flop:

Similar to big pairs, when you flop a set you are in a very profitable situation; perhaps even more so since you have not crippled the deck. When you have a big pair and you make a set, your opponents are less likely to have a hand that will give you any action. In the above example, if you have A-A what hands could your opponents have that will make you money? There is only one ace left in the deck. When your medium pair make a set you are hoping for one or more of your opponents to make top pair. You will win a lot of his chips.

The flop: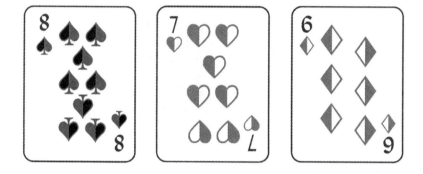

You have flopped an overpair and a straight draw. As you shall see in a moment, you must proceed with caution when your medium pair is an overpair. In this case, however, you have an overpair and a straight draw. You should be aggressive with this hand. You are likely to have the best hand on the flop and in those instances where you do not you have a good possibility of improving to the best hand.

Amber light flops

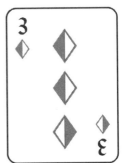

The flop:

When your medium pair is above the board, you probably have the best hand. You can bet or even raise, but be cautious. There are a lot of cards that could come on the turn or river that will beat you. In low-limit hold 'em, players with two overcards will often see the turn. Plus, there is a good chance that one of your low-limit opponents has a hand like small suited connectors which play well on coordinated flops. You are probably the best right now, but you must be prepared to fold if the going gets tough.

The flop:

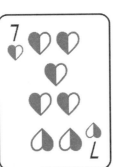

Like big pairs, when there is one overcard to your pair, you will have to go slowly. With experience, you will get a feel for when your medium pair is likely still the best hand. You can bet into one or two opponents but do not generally call bets or raises. If one of your opponents has paired the overcard then you are reduced to two outs. Even if you are the best, it will be hard to feel confident that you are. There is no shame in folding.

The flop:

You have flopped a straight draw. Like any big draw you can continue with the hand. You can even bet the hand if nobody else has since there is some chance that your pocket pair is the best. If it is not, slow down and hope to hit your draw.

Red light flops

The flop:

When you find yourself facing two or more overcards and you do not have a big draw, you should generally check and fold. In particular, with a medium pair in the pocket, overcards will tend to be high cards. Low-limit players love high cards. There is a very good chance that you are drawing to two outs. Fold. Many low-limit players will see the turn or go all the way with their medium pair. They hope that they might still make a set or that their opponent might be bluffing. Do not fall into this trap. If the betting gives you reason to believe you are beat, fold.

Small Pairs

Most low-limit hold 'em players love small pairs. End your love affair with them right now. Small pairs are not very profitable. Under the right circumstances they show a profit, but you must not play them indiscriminately pre-flop and you must not continue with them beyond the flop unless you have a set or a big draw.

Green light flop

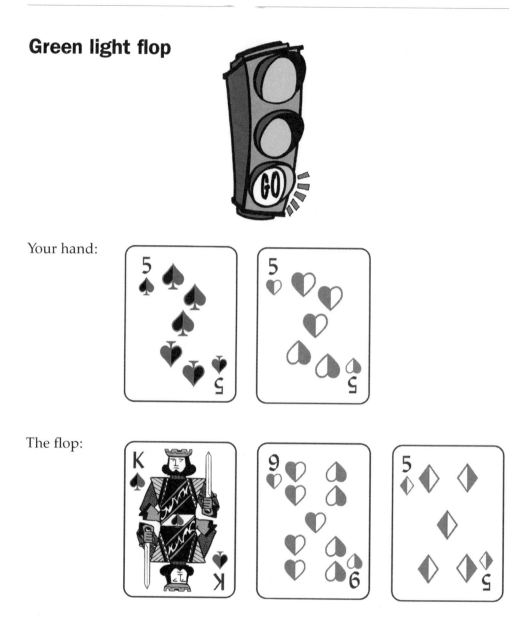

Your hand:

The flop:

Flopping a set is your dream when you have a small pair. You get in cheap and you flop a set. When it happens, you are very likely to win. Be aggressive. It is this phenomenon that causes low-limit players to love small pairs. They remember those times that they won a huge pot when their 3-3 flopped a set. What they do not remember is all those times in which they did not flop a set and lost. Do not get into the habit of always seeing the turn with your pocket pair.

Amber light flops

The flop:

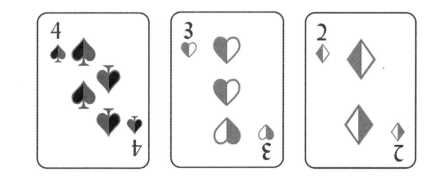

You have an overpair with a straight draw. This will not come along too often with your small pair. You can continue with the hand, but be cautious. If there has been any raising before the flop you are very possibly against a bigger pair. You can continue with the hand, but you are no longer betting or raising with the best - you have a good draw.

The flop:

Like any other big draw you can continue with the hand, but be cautious. You probably need to make your straight to win.

Red light flops

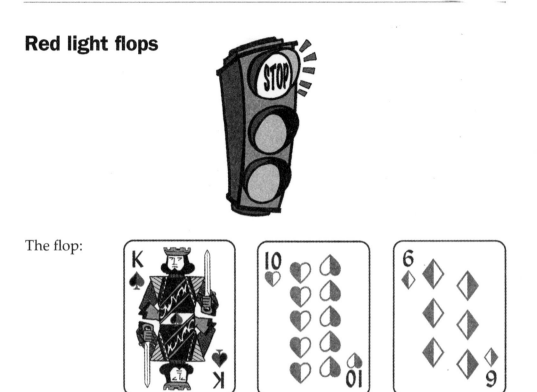

The flop:

Remember, if any of your opponents has a pair above you then you have only two outs. The odds of improving to a set by the river are 10 to 1 against. Fold. Do not take off the turn. Fold on the flop. Small pairs and suited cards are the two kinds of hands that new players and low-limit players overvalue more than any other. With a small pair, if you do not flop a set or a big draw you are finished with the hand. Fold.

Big Aces

One pair is often enough to win in hold 'em. In a sense, big aces are drawing hands. All that you have pre-flop is ace high. You are hoping to flop a pair. If you do, you are in a good position.

Green light flop

Your hand:

The flop:

Leaving aside even bigger flops like K-J-T giving you a nut straight, Q-Q-7 giving you a set with ace kicker, or A-Q-2 giving you two pair, this is exactly the sort of flop you are hoping for with your big ace. You are likely to be in a very profitable situation. Bet and raise. The power of big aces comes from the kicker. If you have A-Q and the flop is Q-Q-7, you have three of a kind with an ace kicker. An opponent who also has a queen is drawing thin. If the board pairs, he or she will win only half the pot. You will get the other half.

Similarly, when you flop only one pair you will have a strong kicker. If you have A-Q and your opponent has K-Q on a flop of Q-T-7, you are a 6 to 1 favorite. Ignoring particularly unusual events, he or she needs to hit his king to win. You are in a very profitable situation. You will win the hand 85% of the time and he or she will rarely fold. He or she may even raise you.

Amber light flops

The flop:

You probably have the best hand, but anytime the flop is coordinated you need to be cautious. With a flop like this there are lots of possibilities for your opponents. A flop like this opens up straight draws, flush draws, two pair, and certainly one pair. If, for example, the flop is Q-J-9 and you are up against one player with A-T and another player with K-J then you will win about 50% of the hands. You have a profitable situation to be sure, but if one of your opponents already has two pair or a straight then you are a long way behind.

The flop:

With two overcards, you may be able to proceed against one or two opponents. If they have both missed the flop you are likely the best. Go ahead and bet. If you have more than two opponents, generally, you should give up. As your number of opponents increase, so does the chance that one of them has already made a pair (or has a pocket pair). If one does, you are reduced to six outs at the best. Very possibly less than that. Low-limit players love aces. If one of your opponents has a pair with an ace kicker you are down to three outs. Overcards is another area in which most low-limit players unnecessarily lose a lot of money. The bottom line is that if you do not flop a pair with your big ace you have missed your hand. Proceed with extreme caution. Against one or two opponents you may still be the best. Against a large number of opponents you are probably drawing thin.

The flop: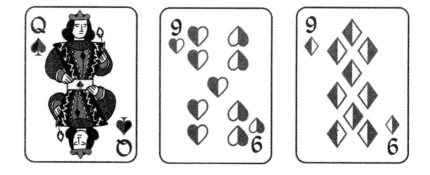

Where you flop top pair and the board is paired, you must again go slow. If one of your opponents has made trips you are drawing to two outs. Proceed with caution. You should probably bet the hand, but if heavy betting breaks out, fold. Most low-limit players will never fold a hand like this. They have top pair with top kicker. It is a through ticket to the river. This is one of the first places that you can learn to fold. If there is lots of raising, or even lots of limping, then *someone* has trips. Fold. You will learn to feel a great sense of pride in folding hands that lesser players refuse to fold. This sort of a situation is one of the easiest spots in which you can learn to do just that.

The flop:

You have flopped second pair with an ace kicker. Like overcards, you might have the best hand. If you do, you are a substantial favorite. If you do not, you are a big dog. Against one or two opponents, you should bet. Against more opponents or facing a bet, folding is probably the best course. Overcard play is another area in which most low-limit players lose more than necessary.

Red light flops

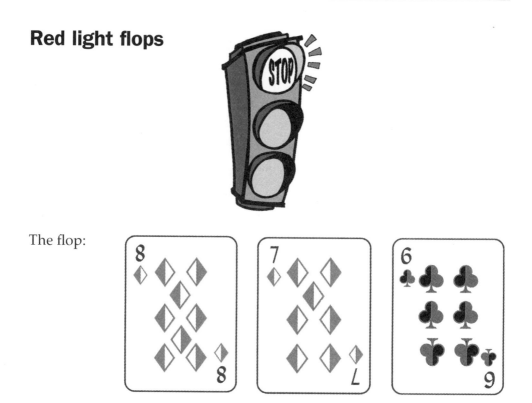

The flop:

With two overcards against a coordinated flop you are in trouble. If one of your opponents has made a pair, you are a 4-1 dog at best. Even if nobody has a pair, it is very likely that one or more of your opponents has a huge draw. In this example, if you are up against one player holding K♦ Q♦ and another player holding J♥ T♥, you will win only 27% of the time. You are not the favorite. The long and the short of it is that when the board is coordinated, you will be a small favorite or a big dog. Generally you should fold.

Suited Aces

Do not fall in love with suited aces. You are hoping to make a flush with your suited aces. You can win if you pair your ace, but you are not likely to get much action unless you are beat.

Green light flops

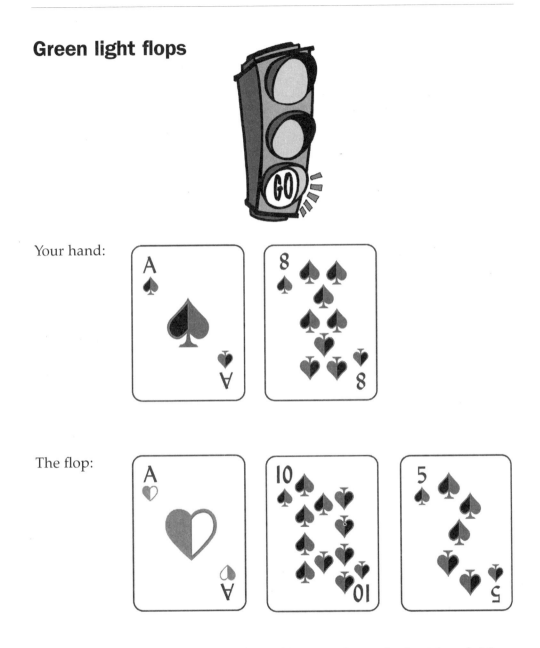

Your hand:

The flop:

You have top pair and a flush draw. You may have the best hand. Many low-limit players will bet or raise with a flush draw. If you bet and someone else raises, it is quite possible that your ace is still the best hand. If it is not, you have nine outs to the nuts (any spade) and an additional three outs for two pair (any eight). This is the sort of flop in which even with a weak kicker you can afford to be quite aggressive.

105

The flop:

You have a flush draw and a straight draw. This is a rare case in which, although you probably do not have the best hand right now, you are the favorite. Anytime you get 15 outs you can be aggressive. If you are against one opponent who holds K♥ K♣ then you will win 62% of the time. With a flop like this to your suited ace, you are a favorite or a very slight dog. The other advantage of playing a hand like this aggressively is that a lot of your low-limit opponents will interpret you as a bluffer. When you cap the betting on the flop with a draw and then river the nut flush, your low-limit opponents will groan and moan. What they do not realize is that when you capped it on the flop, you were the favorite! This is your opportunity to earn a reputation of being a bluffer when you are nothing of the kind. Note, however, that if you do not make your hand on the turn, you are no longer the favorite and you should resort to checking and calling the turn.

Amber light flops

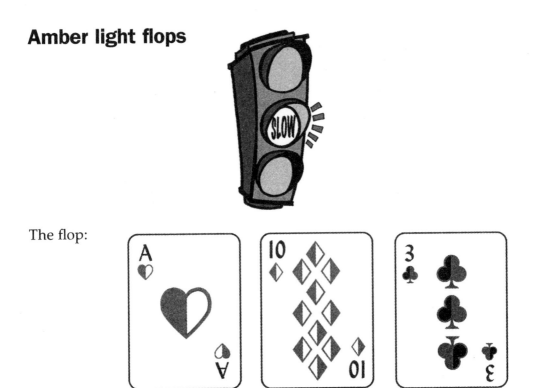

The flop:

You are either a big favorite or a big dog. If you are the only player with an ace and the best that your opponents can muster is one pair or a gutshot, you are in good shape. On the other hand, if you are not the best (someone has a bigger kicker with their ace or has two pair) then you are drawing thin. Practice and experience will guide you in the play of top pair with a weak kicker. Top pair weak-kicker is perhaps *the* hand that you must learn to fold. Experience will teach you when you are likely beat. Most low-limit players will never fold top pair. You must learn to escape from top pair when you are beat.

The flop:

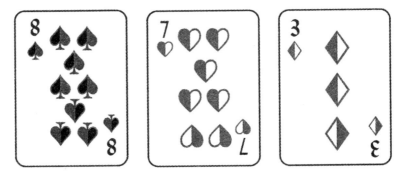

You are quite possibly the best right now, but there are a lot of cards that will beat you. Many players will see the turn when they have two overcards to the board. If you have three or four such opponents against you, there is a mob trying to chase you down. Generally such a hand is worth a bet, but you should be cautious once the turn hits.

The flop:

You have flopped a flush draw. You have actually flopped exactly what you hoped for (I suppose you actually hoped for a complete flush, but that is asking a bit much). Why is this in the amber light category? You are still drawing. Many low-limit players overplay their flush draws. They bet and raise with wild abandoned when they do not, in fact, have the winner. They have a draw. Perhaps they see others betting their flush draws and pick up the habit, or perhaps they have heard of a "semi-bluff." In any event, remember the plan: Bet with the best – Good draw to invest – Fold all the rest. You do not have the best hand, you should not be betting. You have a good draw, you should be calling.

Red light flops

If you flop nothing, check and fold. If you do not have a flush draw, a straight draw, or a pair, give up the hand. Do not "draw for a draw." Do not see the turn hoping to pick up a flush draw or an ace. It will not happen often enough. Fold. You will see your low-limit opponents routinely taking off the turn with as little as one card of their suit. Do not fall prey to this temptation.

Random Big Cards

Another *huge* leak in most low-limit players' games is random big cards. If you fit the flop, you can continue. If you do not, you are finished. Many low-limit players overplay hands like K-Jo before the flop and they hang on too far into the hand. In low-limit hold 'em, random big cards demand a "fit or fold" strategy. Hit the flop or get out.

Green light flops

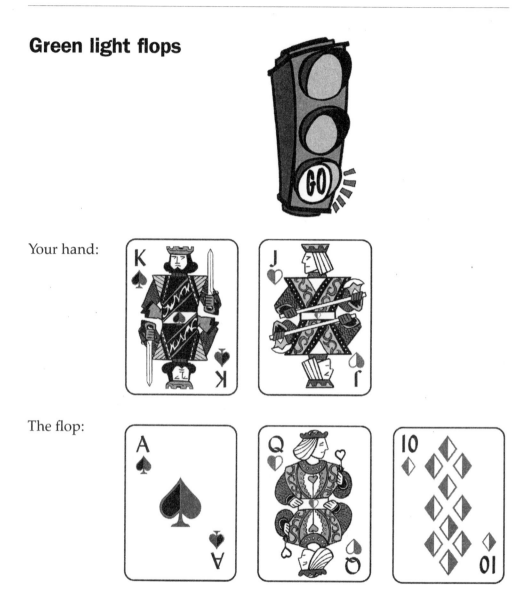

Your hand:

The flop:

You have flopped the nuts. This hand will be very profitable. It is likely that your opponents have caught a piece of the flop, but not as strong as you. A player who has flopped top pair, or even two pair will have a hard time getting away from you.

Amber light flops

The flop:

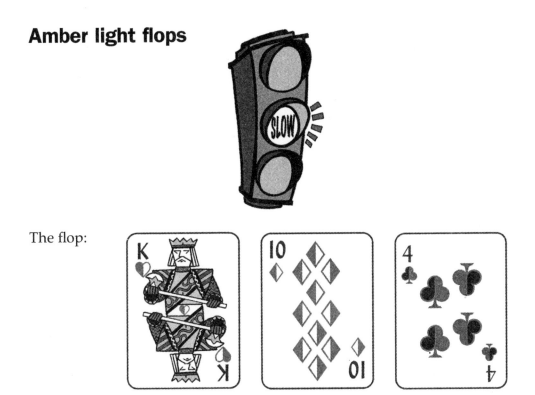

You have flopped top pair, but your kicker is not great. You probably have a profitable hand, but it must be played delicately. One of the skills you must develop is the ability to fold top pair when you are beat. The usual occasion for such an event is when you are up against another top pair and your opponent has a better kicker. This hand is certainly worth a bet and probably even a raise, but if there is heavy betting you must face the question, "Am I beat?" If you are, you are looking at three outs or less. Fold.

Red light flops

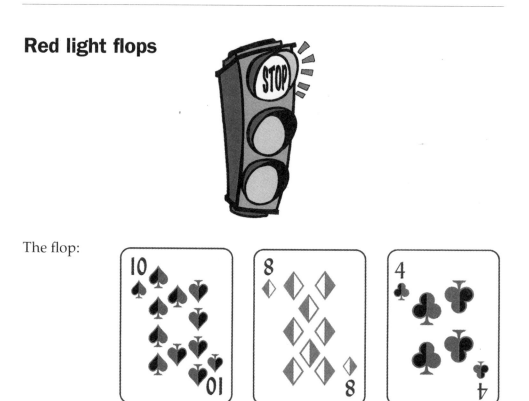

The flop:

Low-limit players love to see the turn with as little as two overcards. Do not fall into this category. With two overcards the very best you can hope for is that you have six outs (any king or any jack). There is little hope that you will win without improving since one or more of your opponents likely has a pair, or at the very least, an ace. Also, there is some likelihood that you have only three outs as either of your overcards could easily be duplicated in an opponent's hand. If one of your opponents has a hand like K-8s then your king is no good to you. If another opponent is calling with two overcards, which happen to be A-Jo, then your jack is no good to you. In almost all circumstances you should abandon your hand when you have two overcards, neither of which is an ace. You are beat and drawing thin.

Small Suited Connectors

Suited connectors are going to need a lot of help to win. Generally you will need to improve to two pair, a straight, or a flush for victory. You are looking for flops that will lead you in that direction.

Green light flops

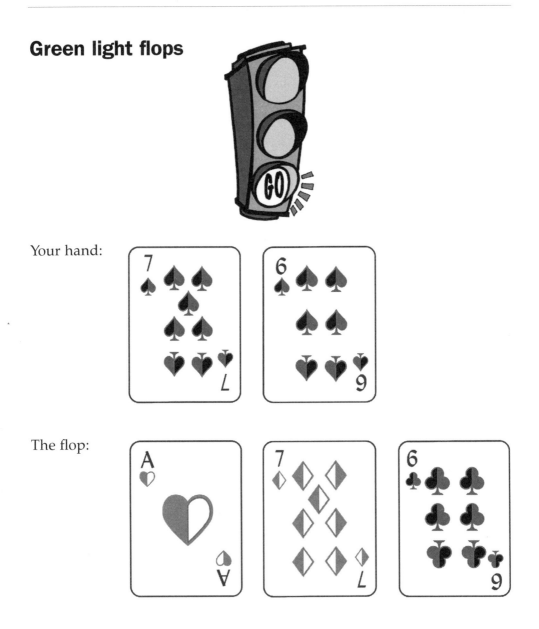

Your hand:

The flop:

When you flop a made hand with your suited connectors you should bet and raise. If you flop a flush or a straight play it aggressively. With a flop like this, you are hoping for a lot of action from a player with a hand like A-K.

One of the problems with small suited connectors is that even when the flop hits you right between the eyes, your hand is still vulnerable. If you flop a flush you do not want to see another flush card on the turn or river since it may make someone a higher flush. If you flop a set, you have a weak kicker. If you flop two pair, the player with top pair has lots of ways to beat you – he or she could draw to either of his pocket cards or the board could pair other than your cards. On the flop, a player with top pair will have five outs (another of the top card or his kicker) and on the turn he or she will have eight outs to beat you (the top card, his kicker, or the other board card).

When the flop hits your suited connectors hard, play the hand aggressively but be prepared to fold on the turn or river if you are beat.

Amber light flops

The flop:

You have flopped a straight draw. Call and try to complete your hand as cheaply as possible. Once you make your hand, be aggressive.

The flop:

You have top pair, but it is small and your kicker is weak. You are probably the best right now, but proceed with caution. There are a lot of cards that will beat you. If you have abided by the starting hand guide, you are playing your small suited connectors against a big field. There will be lots of players trying to chase you down and your hand is far from spectacular.

Red light flops

Fold everything else. Do not "draw for a draw." You will often see low-limit players see the turn or even the river when their small suited connectors flop second pair. If there is betting, you have at best, five outs. You might have less than that. You can only proceed if the pot is very large, which it may be, since you have played your small suited connectors in late position against a large field. If you have the odds to continue you should. Chances are, however, that you will not have sufficient effective odds to continue with the hand and you should fold.

The Turn and River

On the turn, your hand will be even more defined. Did you complete your draw? If you did, instead of calling, you should now be betting and raising. Does the turn card weaken your hand? Perhaps you flopped top pair holding A-8 on a flop of 8-7-5. If the turn is a six or a nine, you should pause.

The same principles that apply on the flop apply on the turn. Bet with the best – good draw to invest – fold all the rest. Because the bet doubles, you need to be sure that you are getting sufficient pot odds to continue your draw. If you made a bad call on the flop, do not compound your problem by making another bad call on the turn.

The river presents a slightly different situation. There are no more cards to come. The basic low-limit poker strategy needs to be altered slightly. If you believe that you have the best hand then bet. When it comes to calling, you are no longer considering a draw, you are considering whether or not the chance of winning the pot is equal to the pot odds being offered. You hold K-Jo, the board is K-T-7-2-9, you have been betting the whole way, bet the river, and your lone opponent raises you. There is $165 in the pot and you have to call $20 to get a showdown. You are getting a little better than 8-1 odds on your call. If you will win one time out of nine, you must call. It will come down to knowing your opponent. Is it possible that he or she has raised with something you can beat? If so, then even a possibility is enough to warrant a call.

Paul closed the book.

"It doesn't look all that hard. How long will it take for me to become a winner?"

"Like most poker questions, the answer to that is," I smiled, "It depends."

Paul nodded, "It depends upon me I suppose?"

"Right. It depends upon whether you can apply the lessons you have learned in the heat of battle. Probably most importantly it initially depends upon whether you can resist temptation. You will be tempted by random suited cards and small pairs. You will be tempted by huge pots that your opponents are winning with hands like 9-6s. You will be tempted by the gambling *demon."*

"The gambling demon?"

"Yes," I nodded gravely, "The gambling demon. He is the same demon that drives people to play slot machines and roulette. The same demon that occasionally drives me to the crap table. The same demon that makes your opponents call two bets cold with hands like 7-4s. Gambling is fun. Pulling in a huge *pot is fun. When you fold you aren't doing either. It is a huge temptation."*

"What can I do to avoid it?" Paul asked.

"You will fall prey to it sometimes I suspect. We all do. What you must do is decide *whether you want to be a weak-willed gambler or a disciplined poker player."*

CHAPTER FIVE

BASIC 7-STUD STRATEGY

Position

The basic principle of position holds true in 7-stud. You have an advantage over players on your right and players on your left have an advantage over you. The difference in 7-stud is that your position in the betting may vary from street to street.

On third street the player with the lowest door card is the forced bring-in. If you are in the number one seat and the number two seat has the bring-in, then you will be last to act. If you are in the number three seat then you will be the second player to act (after the forced bring-in). On fourth street and beyond, the player with the highest up poker hand brings it in. This means the first player to act will possibly change from betting round to betting round. The betting will always flow clockwise, but it can start with a different player each betting round.

A player "to act behind you" refers to a player who has position on you in the current betting round.

Your Starting Hands

As with hold 'em, you are looking for hands that are either the best hand right now, or good draws. Like hold 'em, this book offers a starting hand guide that is slightly tighter than most. The goal is to turn you into a winning player quickly. Starting hand guides are essential for the beginner. Once you are more experienced and have a solid feel for the game, you can take a few additional liberties. In the meantime, start out holding rigidly to these tight starting requirements.

The following table lists a variety of 7-stud match-ups. Again, these are Monte Carlo simulations so they have limited use in the heat of combat. Nevertheless, the table is a convenient way to illustrate the relative strength of hands.

Title	Example	Percentage and Odds	Your Edge
Trips v Under Pair	J♠-J♥-J♣ v T♦-9♣-9♥	93% v 7% 13.3 - 1	Huge Edge
Trips v 3 Flush	J♠-J♥-J♣ v Q♦-7♦-4♦	86% v 14% 6.1 - 1	Huge Edge
Trips v Over pair	J♠-J♥-J♣ v A♦-K♥-K♣	85% v 15% 5.7 - 1	Huge Edge
Pair v Three random cards	J♠-J♥-T♣ v X-X-X	70% v 30% 2.3 - 1	Big Edge
Pair v Three straight with no over	J♠-J♥-T♣ v 8♠-7♥-6♦	68% v 32% 2.1 - 1	Big Edge
Pair v Three flush with no over	J♠-J♥-T♣ v 9♦-7♦-4♦	65% v 35% 1.9 - 1	Big Edge
Pair v Three over	J♠-J♥-T♣ v A♠-K♥-Q♦	64% v 36% 1.8 - 1	Small Edge
Pair v Smaller Pair with undercard kicker	J♠-J♥-T♣ v 9♠-9♥-8♦	62% v 38% 1.6 - 1	Small Edge
Pair v Three flush with one over	J♠-J♥-T♣ v Q♦-7♦-4♦	60% v 40% 1.5 - 1	Small Edge
Pair v Three straight with one over	J♠-J♥-T♣ v Q♠-J♥-T♦	60% v 40% 1.5 - 1	Small Edge
Pair v Smaller Pair with overcard kicker	J♠-J♥-T♣ v 9♠-9♥-K♦	58% v 42% 1.4 - 1	Small Edge
Pair v Three card straight flush	J♠-J♥-T♣ v 8♦-7♦-6♦	56% v 44% 1.2 - 1	Negligible Edge

Unlike hold 'em, it is difficult to get a huge edge (defined as at least 4-1). You will only get a huge edge in 7-stud when you start with a set. You get a set once every 425 hands (referred to as being "rolled up"). Thus, you do not get a huge edge very often in 7-stud.

A big edge (defined as 2-1) arises when a pair goes up against either three random cards or a straight draw with all three cards lower than the pair. For convenience, (not quite 2-1 but close) a pair versus a flush draw with all three cards lower than the pair is also considered a big edge. The lesson is that you should not enter the fray indiscriminately. Some low-limit 7-stud players will routinely call on the cheap streets (3rd and 4th) looking to develop a hand. Do not get into this habit. If you are up against a pair, you are probably giving up a big edge. Similarly, you should not routinely play any three straight cards or any three flush cards because if all three of your cards are below your opponent's pair, you are giving up a big edge.

Finally, the majority of 7-stud confrontations will fall into the "small edge" category. You, or your opponent, has a pair and the other player has a smaller pair or a drawing hand with at least one overcard to the pair. The lesson, however, should be obvious. You want to be the player with the biggest pair. Regardless of whether you are against a smaller pair or a draw, you will have an edge between 1.9-1 and 1.4-1.

Also, note the importance of overcards. A pair versus a flush draw with no overcards to the pair will win 65% of the time. If the flush draw has one overcard, the pair is reduced to 60%. If the flush draw has three overcards, the pair only wins about 50% of the time. Overcards matter a great deal. You must pay attention to all three cards in your hand.

Finally, a negligible edge occurs anytime a pair goes up against a straight flush draw.

Live Cards

Just as overcards are important in 7-stud, live cards are also important. In hold 'em the only cards that you get to see are your own cards and the board. In 7-stud, you get to see all of your opponents' boards. This means that there are a lot more cards to consider. In short, you will have a better idea how many "outs" you have. In the following table you have (Q♣-7♣)-4♣. The game is 7 handed. The row "0 clubs out" means that none of your opponents show a club as their door card. "1 club out" means that one of your opponents has a club as his door card and so on. All players go to the river every hand and their hands are random except for the club that they have been assigned as their door card.

Q♣-7♣-4♣

Clubs you can see	Percentage
0 clubs out	20.8% winner
1 club out	19.4% winner
2 clubs out	17.9% winner
3 clubs out	16.7% winner
4 clubs out	15.1% winner
5 clubs out	13.8% winner
6 clubs out	12.6% winner

This is by no means a scientific example, but it is sufficient to illustrate the point. The more of your suit that you can see, the poorer your hand. In the example, if you can see 5 clubs among your opponents' door cards then your expectation is below that of a random hand, despite the fact that you have started with a three flush.

Principle: *7-stud is a game of live cards. The more of your cards that are live, the better.*

Your Hand is Relative to Your Opponent's

Note that in 7-stud the strength of your hand is best measured relative to the strength of your opponent's board. If you have a pair of aces but your opponent shows trip sevens, you *know* that you are beat. If you play aces against (X-X)-8-7-6-5 then you should be very worried that your opponent has a straight. On the other hand, if you play aces against (X-X)-K-7-5-2, you will have more confidence that you are still the best. You must pay careful attention to your opponent's board cards and how strong your hand is *relative* to what you see.

Bet with the best – Good draw to invest
– Fold all the rest.

You want to start with the best hand or a good draw. Generally you are looking for a big pair on third street, or a good "live" draw against multiple opponents. Let's look at various starting hands and decide how to play them.

Trips

As stated, you will only be dealt trips once every 425 hands. Not too often. When you do get them you are in a very profitable situation. There is almost no doubt that you have the best hand. The basic low-limit poker strategy tells you to bet or raise, and I recommend you do just that. Keep betting or raising throughout the hand until you are given a very good reason to believe that you are beat.

You might slow down if one of your opponents looks like they have made a straight or a flush. Also, you might slow down if one of your opponents has paired his door card and it is higher than your trips. Many low-limit 7-stud players will play any pair. If they started with a pair in their first three cards, there is about a two-thirds chance that their starting pair will match their door card. The three possibilities for a starting pair are (7-7)-K, (7-K)-7, and (K-7)-7. In all three instances there is a pair of sevens, and two-thirds of the time the doorcard is a seven. Beware the paired door card, it often means that your low-limit opponent has made trips.

If you feel that one of your opponents has you beat, it does not mean that you should fold. When you start with trips, you will make a full house about one time in three. If you are overtaken you are no longer the best, but in most circumstances you will have more than enough pot odds to draw for a full house or quads.

A Pair Bigger than Any Card You See

If you have a pair that outranks your remaining opponents' door cards then you very probably have the best hand. There is some risk that one of your opponents has trips or a pair in the hole that is bigger than your pair, but you must not live in fear. When you have a pair that is bigger than any remaining visible card – bet or raise. Go back to the table showing hand match-ups. Ideally, you will find yourself heads up against one opponent who has a smaller pair or a draw. In this case you will have at least a small edge and very possibly a big edge.

Note that I said "you have a pair that outranks your *remaining* opponents' doorcards." If you start with a pair of jacks and one of your opponents has a king doorcard but he or she has folded, then you meet the criterion of having "a pair bigger than any card you can see." Do not count doorcards that have folded as "cards you can see."

If you get two or three callers, you may find yourself in the position we have previously discussed. You are the favorite, but you will probably lose. For instance, if you start with (9♠-9♠)-A♦ and you are against two opponents who have (7♠-7♠)-8♦ and (Q♣-6♣)-4♣ respectively, you will win 40%, the sevens will win 27%, and the clubs will win 33%. You are the favorite, but you will *probably* lose. Get used to it: that is low-limit poker. It is still a very profitable situation and you should not be deterred from betting.

Not only is it desirable to have the biggest pair that you can see, it is also desirable that your pair be as big as possible. A pair of aces is superior to a pair of jacks. This should be obvious to you. Although a pair of jacks may be the highest pair on 3rd street, a single card could land on one of your opponent's hands to give him a bigger pair (any queen, king, or ace). If you start with a pair of aces, it is impossible for a single card to make a higher pair for an opponent. The lower your pair, the more likely that your opponents will have overcards to your pair. Indeed, three overcards are only a 1.8-1 dog to a pair. If your pair is aces, it is not possible for your opponents to have overcards and you are that much stronger.

Also, there is an advantage to your pair being concealed. When your pair is split, then you make trips when you pair your doorcard. If your pair is buried, then what looks like an innocuous card to your opponents may give you trips.

If you have a pair bigger than any card you can see, you likely have the best hand and you should bet or raise.

One Card is Bigger Than Your Pair

You can also enter the fray when there is one remaining card bigger than your pair. Do so only if all your cards are live. In other words, if you have two tens and there is only one doorcard among your remaining opponents that is larger than a ten, you can bet or raise if you have not seen another ten, or another card matching your kicker.

This will occur in one of two ways. Suppose you have a pair of tens. There is a king to act before the action reaches you. If the king limps in, you can play. It is not impossible for him to have a pair of kings, but his limp-in tends to indicate weakness making it more likely that your pair of tens is the best right now.

Similarly, if the action reaches you and there is a king behind you, go ahead and raise. He or she might have another king, but chances are that he or she does not.

Note also that all your cards must be live. This means that you have not seen any cards among your opponents' doorcards that will improve your hand. If you hold (T-K)-T then you must not have seen another ten or king. Live cards are *very* important in 7-stud. For example, suppose the action is three way, you have (T-K)-T, one of your opponents has (Q-Q)-7, and the other has a random hand. In this case, you will win 36% of the time, the queens will win 44% of the time, and the random hand 20% of the time in a Monte Carlo simulation. Run the same simulation but give the random hand a K as his doorcard and the winning percentages become 33% for you, 45% for the queens and 22% for the random hand. Both the queens and the random hand have gained at your expense.

None of this should be taken as suggesting that you should play your pair against one card bigger than your pair if you *know* that you are beat. The situations I have just described attempt to balance the likelihood that you have the best hand against the possibility that you do not. You are probably the best, but if you are not then you are not that far behind.

Principle: *In 7-stud, you are looking for the type of hand that is* **probably** *the best, but if it is not, you have a live draw to become the best.*

Straight Flush Draw

You can play straight flush draws. In the match-up table, a pair will beat a three card straight flush 1.2-1. Assuming you hold (7♥-6♥)-5♥ and your opponent holds an overpair, you are a dog. The advantage to you comes from the fact that you can fold early in the hand if you are not developing a winner. Your opponent with a pair will have difficulty folding and you will usually get paid off all the way to the river on those occasions that you draw out on him.

On third street you have (7♥-6♥)-5♥ and your opponent has a pair of jacks. On 4th street you receive the T♣. You fold. You have lost only one bet. Even if you go to 5th street before you give up you will have lost only two small bets. When you do develop a hand superior to your opponent's, he or she will have difficulty releasing his pair and you will win big bets from him on later streets.

Live cards matter here as well. In this case, you are interested in how many of your suit are among your opponents' cards and how many of your straight cards are among your opponents' cards. Straight cards count as being within two of your starting hand. So, in the example of you holding (7♥-6♥)-5♥, your live straight cards are 9, 8, 4 and 3.

Similarly, the overall rank of your straight flush draw matters. (Q♥-J♥)-T♥ is better than (7♥-6♥)-5♥ because of the extra possibilities presented by the high ranks. Spiking a pair as high as a queen may be enough to win, whereas a small pair like a five is possibly no help.

Flush Draw

Look back at the match-up table. A flush draw will win 35 to 40% against a pair heads up. Simply put, you do not want to play flush draws heads up against a pair. Low-limit 7-stud players commonly play *any* flush draw in *any* situation. This is a bad idea. To play flush draws, you need to have two or more overcards to your opponent's pair, or you need more than one opponent. I call this my "flush draw rule of two." Either you have *two or more overcards* to your opponent's apparent pair or you have *two or more opponents*.

From the match-up table you know that if you play (J♠ -J♥)-T♦ v (Q♦-7♦)-4♦ the flush draw will win 40% of the time. If you add a third hand, (9♣-9♠)-A♥ the flush draw will win 33% of the time. The addition of one other hand makes the flush draw with one overcard an even money proposition. You have about a one-third chance of winning the pot, and you will be able to fold if your hand does not develop. Your opponents with pairs will have trouble folding.

Again, you must consider how live your draw is. Are there any of your suit already gone in your opponents' doorcards? In the above example, if we substitute some suits so that the hands are (J♠-J♦)-T♦, (9♣-9♦)-A♦ and (Q♦-7♦)-4♦, the flush draw will only win about 20%. Four of your diamonds are used up in your opponents' hands and you are no longer even money.

On third street play "good" flush draws and fold "bad" flush draws. A good flush draw will be either (1) Heads up where you have at least two overcards to your opponent's apparent pair; or (2) You have at least two opponents. In either case, no more than two of your suit are used up in any of your opponents' doorcards. Bad flush draws are, therefore, small flush draws played heads up or any flush draw with three of more of your suit dead.

Principle: *7-stud is a game of live cards. The more of your cards that are live, the better.*

Straight Draw

Like flush draws, most low-limit 7-stud players will play *any* straight draw in *any* circumstance. This is a huge mistake. To play straight draws you need multiple opponents. Heads up against a pair a straight will win about 40% of the time. You are a dog. Fold.

What if we add a second opponent like we did with a flush draw? If the hands are (J♠-J♥)-T♦, (8♠-7♥)-6♦, and (5♠-5♥)-A♦ then the straight draw will only win about 20% of the time. Even with two opponents you are a dog.

Like a flush draw, your hand is only good if your cards are live. The cards you are looking for are within two from either end of your three card straight. If your hand is (8-7)-6, you are interested in tens, nines, fives, and fours. If more than two of these cards are dead, you cannot proceed under any circumstances.

Principle: *On third street play "good" straight draws and fold "bad" straight draws.*

On third street a "good" straight draw will meet the following criterion: (1) at least three opponents; and (2) no more than two of the cards you need are among your opponents' doorcards. Bad straight draws, therefore, will be any straight draw played against one or two opponents, or any straight draw where three for more of your required cards are dead.

Big Cards

If you have three cards ten or above, you are deemed to have "big cards." A look back at the table shows that three big cards (all three over the opposing pair) will win about 40% of the time. Like other drawing hands, you do not want to play three big cards heads up against a probable pair. Can you ever play big cards?

You will not be giving up too much if you *always* fold three big cards. On the other hand, when you are dealt three big cards, you will frequently have the highest door card. If you have the highest doorcard and nobody has limped-in or raised, then go ahead and complete the bet. Your hope is that you will win the antes and the bring-in bet right there. In a typical low-limit 7-stud game, however, you will be called by players with hands even worse than yours. Proceed with caution. You are bluffing. If you do get called, you are probably a 3-2 dog, but you might improve and win the hand.

Fold all the Rest

Everything else is junk. Fold on third street. Many of your little-skilled low-limit 7-stud opponents will play many more hands than that. Do not fall prey to the temptation. Start with the best hand or start with a good draw. Although your little-skilled opponents will win all sort of pots, they are starting with poor draws. In the long run, they are losing players.

Fourth Street

If you still have reason to believe that you have the best hand, keep with the basic low-limit poker strategy and bet. If you started with a draw, your rule of thumb for fourth street is *improve or fold*. Your three flush is now, hopefully, a four flush. Your three straight is now, hopefully, a four straight. If not, then fold. The exception is against three or more opponents. If you do not improve your drawing hand on 4th street but you are still facing three or more opponents, go ahead and call once more. Do not call a raise but if you can see 5th street for one more bet you probably should. You are hoping to improve your hand on 5th street.

Fifth Street and Beyond

The bet doubles on fifth street. Here, even more than fourth street, your decision to continue is crucial. If you decide to continue with the hand, you *will* call again on sixth street since there will be even more money in the pot and only one card to come.

The tricky part to 7-stud is that in order to make a proper pot odds calculation, you need to track not only the number of your outs that are still "live" but also the number of cards that you have not seen. If you have a flush draw you should know how many of your suit are gone. If you have a straight draw then how many of your straight cards are gone? 5th street is the time to decide if you have enough outs to continue to the river. Generally, if you have a four flush or an open straight you can keep drawing.

One other critical issue is the size of your draw. If you are going past 5th street with a drawing hand then you want to have a bigger draw than the competition. On fifth street, if you have a four card straight and you are up against one player who has two pair and another player who has a flush draw, you should frequently fold. You must not only make your hand, your opponents must *miss theirs*. Similarly, if you hold a small pair with overcards and you are against an overpair and a flush draw, you should fold. Again, you find yourself in the position of needing to make your hand *and* have the flush draw miss *and* have the overpair not improve. You must considerably devalue your draw if you are against better draws.

If you decide that you have the best hand or a good draw on 5th street then you are in for the ride. For sixth and seventh street simply follow the basic low-limit poker strategy: Bet with the best – Good draw to invest – Fold all the rest. If you started with a high pair and you are raised by an opponent who shows a four flush, fold. Do not get married to a hand simply because you started out as the best. You must be willing to fold hands when you are overtaken and you have few outs left with which to win.

"If I am going to specialize in one game," Paul asked, "which should it be?"

"Hold 'em, " I suggested, "It is long and away the more popular of the two. If you are going to concentrate on only one, learn hold 'em and you will be much more likely to find a game."

"Why is it more popular? When we played as kids we played all sort of variations of 7-stud."

I nodded. "Hold 'em is faster. There are more hands per hour."

"I like faster," Paul grinned.

"Most people seem to," I agreed. "Also, despite the fact that 7-stud has one extra betting round, hold 'em has more betting and raising than 7-stud. There is just more action in most hold 'em games."

"I like action," Paul was beaming now.

I nodded. "Also, limit hold 'em offers the best chance for weak players to beat their more skilled opponents. That is why you can always find a hold 'em game. It takes the weak players a lot longer to figure out that they are weak players because the natural variance of the game will frequently deliver a winning session."

PLAYER CLASSIFICATION

So far we have considered hold 'em and 7-stud as though they are played according to some rote method. If you play tight initially, bet when you have the best, and call with a good draw, you will be a winning player in almost any low-limit game. This is true. For the most part, it is true because low-limit poker is a card game. Acquire the best cards and bet. There is, however, an undercurrent; an undercurrent that takes on more and more importance as you go up in limits and play against more and more skilled opponents. An undercurrent that becomes a tsunami once you reach the level of world class play. As Doyle Brunson says in *Super System*: "Poker is a game of people. That is the most important lesson you will learn from my book."

You can play by rote against low-limit opponents because in any low-limit game, there will be enough weak opponents that you will be a winner despite the presence of a *few* skilled players. Ultimately, however, you will need to learn to "read" your opponents. You can increase your profits in low-limit games by learning to classify your opponents, quickly and accurately. If you hope to play at higher limits this skill will prove essential.

This chapter gives you a player classification system. Ken Buntjer's book *The Secret to Winning Big in Tournament Poker* also supplies a thorough player classification system. You will often hear "rock, fish, and maniac" as player types, but Buntjer is much more thorough. This chapter, too, attempts to be more complete.

The point of player classification is to (1) define the range of hands that your opponent might hold; and (2) select an optimum strategy against each player class.

Player Types

Although it is convenient to talk about player types, it is important to note that no two players are *exactly* alike. When we define player types, we are really defining behaviors that *tend* to group together. In other words, if player type "A" makes error type "X," then he or she will *tend* to also make errors "Y" and "Z." It is not necessarily the case, but it is a reasonable gamble to take.

Note that each of the player types has a particular error that they make with the greatest frequency. This means, once you have classified a player, you can exploit his weakness by employing tactics that work particularly well against the particular mistake his type most frequently makes.

Player categories and most common mistakes are as follows: *Fish* call too often, *Rocks* do not call often enough, and *Maniacs* bet and raise too often. The error of "calling too often" is the most common mistake. One category does not deal adequately with players who call too often. Thus, Fish subdivides into three categories: *Screaming Fish, Over-value Tuna, and Deep Sea Bass.* There is a sixth and final category of player. The one that you want to be. The type of player that does not make mistakes – the *Fox.*

In addition to the kinds of errors that players are likely to make, each player type also has a varying amount of ability to think about what cards you have. At the far left of the continuum we find the noble Screaming Fish (S-Fish) who has *no ability whatsoever* to consider your hand. S-Fish can only see his own cards. He or she plays according to some odd set of self-inflicted rules about what are good hands and bad hands. What their opponent may have will have no bearing at all on how they play their own hand. At the other end of the scale is the Fox. The Fox thinks *more* about your hand than his or her own. He or she is interested in winning the pot by any and every means at his disposal.

In a nutshell, players are on a continuum in accordance with the following:

S-Fish	O-Tuna	Rock	D-Bass	Fox
X	X	X	X	X

No idea what you have -->---->---->---->---->Some Idea -->---->---->---->---->Very good idea what you have

The Screaming Fish (S-Fish)

Screaming Fish is the first of the three kinds of fish. S-Fish is the grist of the poker mill. Players of this type are the biggest losers of all. S-Fish has very little understanding of hand value. He or she does not have any idea how good his hand is relative to the probable winning hand. For instance, in hold 'em S-Fish might think that flopping bottom pair in a three handed pot is pretty good: after all, he or she has a pair! Also, S-Fish has no ability to consider your hand. Having flopped bottom pair in a three handed pot he refuses to fold even though there is a bet and three raises. At the river, S-Fish calls all bets and is surprised to learn that the player who re-re-raised on the turn has a set.

The primary error of the S-Fish is to call too much. S-Fish will *not* give up on a hand. If there is any possibility that he or she has the best hand or might develop the best hand, he or she will simply fasten the seatbelt and come along for the ride. He has A-3 in hold 'em and the flop is J-7-2? No problem for the S-Fish, he or she will see the turn hoping to spike an ace.

Here is a list of common mistakes that the S-Fish will make. If you see a player make these errors you can classify him or her as an S-Fish:

1. Limping in with complete crap. In hold 'em, this might include hands like T-4s or 8-6o. In 7-stud, this might include hands like (A-7)-4 or (K-Q)-8.

2. Calling a raise pre-flop with complete crap. In hold 'em, this might include random suited cards or connected offsuit cards. In 7-stud, it might include two suited cards or an ace with two random cards.

3. Calling past the flop in hold 'em or past 5th street in 7-stud with any drawing hand like gutshots, a solo ace, 3 flush, and small pair to name a few.

4. Paying off the river *everytime*. If S-Fish makes it to the river, you can count on him to call. You will not bluff him out.

5. Any other *grotesque* error that you can think of. If you ever find yourself thinking, "How did he or she call with *that*???" then you probably have an S-Fish on your hands.

It is easy to imagine the S-Fish's thought process. He or she sees a hand like T-4s in hold 'em and thinks, "I have the first two parts to a flush I can't stop now." In 7-stud he or she finds (J-8)-7 and thinks, "All I need is a ten and a nine and I have a straight." S-Fish loves potential. He or she imagines all the possibilities the cards offer and pursues the slimmest of them.

To win chips from an S-Fish you will need to have the best hand. Just as S-Fish cannot put you on a hand, neither can you put S-Fish on anything. He or she is essentially bluff proof because he or she has a huge calling range. You will beat S-Fish with the basic low-limit poker strategy. You will beat S-Fish by acquiring the best hand and betting it. S-Fish will call with all sort of lesser hands and you will win the money.

Thus, you can be more liberal in the cards that you will play when you are up against S-Fish. Since you know that he or she will play almost any two cards and pay you off if he or she has anything at all, you can go looking for a hand more often. If you miss the flop in hold 'em or fail to develop anything by 5th street in 7-stud, stop betting. Fold if he or she bets. On the other hand, if you have something, go ahead and bet. A middle pair in 7-stud is worth betting. Second or even third pair in hold 'em is worth betting.

Finally, S-Fish tends to be passive. If S-Fish is raising then it is likely that he or she has a strong hand. S-Fish does not understand hand value. Generally he or she deals with this lack of understanding by going into "call mode." But, even S-Fish understands the nuts. If S-Fish is raising, beware, he or she probably has a big hand.

The Over Value Tuna (O-Tuna)

O-Tuna is the most common player in low-limit poker. He or she has a vague idea of hand value. In hold 'em, he or she will certainly understand that top pair on the flop is decent. In 7-stud, he or she will understand that having a pair higher than any card he or she can see is a good starter. O-Tuna's understanding, however, is vague and he or she tends to overvalue drawing hands (thus the "over value" moniker). He or she has little or no ability to consider what you have. Like S-Fish, O-Tuna plays his or her own cards. He or she loves suited cards. He or she will play *any* three suited cards in 7-stud and will certainly believe that a hand like J-7s can be played in early position in hold 'em.

Like S-Fish, the primary error that O-Tuna makes is to call too much. He or she overvalues big cards, suited cards, medium pair, and small pair. He or she is more selective than S-Fish, but he or she still calls too much. In hold 'em he or she will call a raise with K-Jo. He or she might even raise in hold 'em with a hand like K-J. He or she is not bluffing. He thinks of K-J as a powerful hand and he or she is not afraid to raise with it.

Here is a list of errors that O-Tuna frequently makes. If you see a player make these mistakes you can classify that player as O-Tuna:

1. In hold 'em, calling two bets cold with random big cards that are *not* a big ace. For example, calling two cold with hands like K-J, Q-J, or J-T.

2. In hold 'em or 7-stud, calling two bets cold with a small pair.

3. Limping in with big cards – in hold 'em hands like K-To and in 7-stud hands like (A-Q)-9.

4. Playing big suited cards or suited connectors in hold 'em and three suited cards in 7-stud, regardless of position or number of bets. Hands like Q-8s or 6-5s in hold 'em and (9-7)-2 suited in 7-stud.

5. Calling with moderate hands. In hold 'em O-Tuna will tend to go into "call-mode" with a hand like second pair. In 7-stud O-Tuna will tend to go into "call-mode" with two small pair against a visible big pair.

It is easy to imagine O-Tuna's thought process. O-Tuna likes big cards because he or she has learned that big pairs are powerful holdings in both hold 'em and 7-stud. Thus, O-Tuna cannot lay down a hand like K-J because he or she might flop a big pair. O-Tuna has not learned that not all big cards are created equal. He or she likes to draw for flushes because when you hit a flush you can win a big pot. O-Tuna loves to go looking with small pair because he or she has won some huge pots when they turn into sets.

Similar to S-Fish, to win chips from O-Tuna you need to have the best hand. His primary mistake is calling too much. Acquire the best hand and bet it. Once O-Tuna enters a pot he or she will often go too far. In hold 'em, O-Tuna will take off the turn with as little as one overcard and then fold. In 7-stud he or she may call on 5th street with as little as three suited cards. In either case, O-Tuna has entered the pot with what he or she considers to be a quality starting hand and thus, is reluctant to give it up. O-Tuna can be bluffed, but only where he or she considers himself to have nothing. If O-Tuna enters the pot with a hand like 6-5s in hold 'em and completely misses the flop, he or she will fold.

You can loosen up slightly against O-Tuna. You know that he or she will play any pair and will pay you off to the river with them. Thus, you can go looking to develop a hand slightly more frequently than usual. There is a good chance of getting paid off when you develop the best hand.

Finally, also like S-Fish, O-Tuna is generally passive. He or she is not a habitual bluffer. If O-Tuna is betting or raising with a hand that does not warrant such bets, it is because he or she *thinks* that it is the best hand – not because he or she is bluffing. Facing aggression, O-Tuna will usually go into "call-mode." The exception is that O-Tuna will often bet his drawing hands. In hold 'em, when flopping a four flush, O-Tuna will bet. In 7-stud, with a flush draw on 3rd street, he or she will bet.

S-Fish and O-Tuna are found in huge schools in low-limit poker games, which is precisely why the basic low-limit poker strategy works.

The Rock

A fair number of players eventually become Rocks. In fact, Rocks are profitable players in low-limit poker games. Recall the story of Cowboy Carl? Carl, the ultimate rock, is a marginally profitable player. Rocks have some understanding of hand value. Mostly, they have learned to recognize very strong hands. They are not able to extract maximum value from their marginal hands. Like fish, they have very limited ability to think about your cards. What ability they do have, they ignore. After all, they have been waiting all day to get a pair of aces. They are not about to fold them just because there has been a raise and a re-raise on the turn.

"It seems to me that the basic low-limit poker strategy you prescribe will make me into a Rock," Paul stated.

"Yes it will," I agreed.

"So Rocks are good players?" he asked.

"Rocks are profitable players as long as they are facing weak opposition," I answered. "There are lots of professional players who are Rocks. They eke out a living by seeking out games with weak opponents, but if they try to play against Foxes they get killed."

Paul was not happy, "Then why are you teaching me to be a Rock?"

"First, it is easy to be a Rock and make money. Second, it is a good stopping point along the road towards being a Fox. Walk before you can run."

The primary error of Rocks is that they do not call often enough. They do not play enough hands and they do not play them aggressively enough. Rocks are willing to wait and wait and wait for a really good starting hand. In hold 'em, Rocks are looking for a big pair or a big ace. In 7-stud, they are looking for a big pair or a big draw. Rocks will fold too often early in a hand. If you face a Rock in the big-blind in hold 'em, you should frequently attack his or her blind. If there is a Rock behind you in 7-stud with a big door card you can attack – he or she probably does not have a big pair. If the Rock *does*, he or she will call or raise, and you will know to escape the hand with a minimum loss. A word of warning: once a Rock decides to play a hand, he or she will be hard to shake. When a Rock enters the fray, he or she is often reluctant to give up.

A Rock's betting tends to reflect the exact value of his or her hand. If he or she is limping, he or she wants to see the next cards cheaply. Small pairs are a typical example. When a Rock enters a pot with a raise you *get out of the way*. Let the Rock have it. He or she has a good hand and it is *very* hard to get the Rock to release it. After all, he or she has waited for one and a half hours to get this hand, he or she is not going to fold it.

Here is a list of errors that a Rock typically makes. If you see a player making these plays you may classify that player as a Rock:

1. Plays *substantially* fewer hands than the table average.

2. In hold 'em, he or she rarely defends his big blind and he or she does not like random big cards that do not include an ace (e.g. K-J, Q-J, etc).

3. Never shows down a bluff.

4. He or she does not like drawing hands. In hold 'em he or she avoids hands like 8-7s in any circumstance. In 7-stud he or she avoids hands like (T-9)-8 offsuit.

5. His or her play is predictable.

The Rock believes that if you start with the best hand, you ought to finish with the best hand. Furthermore, a Rock likes to feel *certain* that he or she has the best hand. Rocks do not like uncertainty. This is why he or she hates hands like K-J in hold 'em. Rocks want to know *right now* where he or she stands. Rocks want to start with a lead and have it hold up.

Early in the hand, Rocks will play too tight. In hold 'em, you should frequently steal a Rock's blinds. He or she will not defend often enough. When a Rock does defend the blind and misses the flop, then he or she will frequently fold to a bet. On the other hand, if the Rock calls on the flop, he or she will not let it go. If you can bluff the Rock, it will be early in the hand. If the Rock reaches the latter betting streets then you *know* that he or she has something. Generally speaking, do not try to bluff a Rock late in a hand.

In the early stages of a hand, loosen up and raise. Bluff him. See if you can get him to fold his marginal hands. Beware though that if your early bluff fails you must give up that tactic. Also, if it is early in a hand and a Rock is betting or raising then you should fold all but your best holdings. Aggression from a Rock early in a hand means that he or she has a good hand and he or she is unlikely to release it. Get out of his way and wait for your next opportunity to steal his money or beat him with a better hand. Bluff him or get a better hand and make him pay.

Finally, Rocks are generally predictable and timid. His or her betting is reflective of the quality of his or her hand. Rocks bet when they have the best; they check and call with their draws.

The Deep Sea Bass (D-Bass)

D-Bass is a deep thinking fish – a fish to be sure but not without skill. He or she has a complete knowledge of hand value and is able to give a lot of consideration to your hand. However, D-Bass often gives too much credit to his or her own ability and to the other players. Like other species of fish, D-Bass calls too much.

143

D-Bass plays too many hands. D-Bass believes he or she can outplay the other players. He or she has read all the books, played poker at home on the computer, understands pot odds, and likes to bluff. D-Bass is the most complex player category and the one with the widest variation from player to player.

Here is a list of errors that D-Bass typically makes. If you see a player make these errors you may classify that player as D-Bass:

1. He or she has a betting reflex. If you check, he or she bets.

2. He or she frequently makes a "free card play" (raising in late position early in a hand hoping that you will check on a later street and give him or her a "free" card).

3. He or she frequently re-raises with small pair in both hold 'em and 7-stud.

4. He or she is frequently caught bluffing.

5. He or she will often talk about what a good player he or she is.

The D-Bass believes that he or she can outplay the other players. D-Bass believes that a high level of skill will overcome loose starting standards. Mike Caro would refer to D-Bass as having *Fancy Play Syndrome.* That is to say that D-Bass simply cannot resist making a move. D-Bass is often, however, made a loser because he or she will give the other players too much credit for advanced thinking. D-Bass calls too much, mostly because he or she fears that you are putting a move on. D-Bass is a fancy play artist that thinks that you are too.

You will beat D-Bass by refusing to fold your marginal hands and playing your good hands with extreme aggression. His or her bets and raises are frequently out of line, which means you can play a few more cards than you otherwise might. You are looking to develop a hand because D-Bass will stay in too long. In the later stages of a hand you should not lay down your marginal holdings. In hold 'em, if a Rock is betting and you have top pair with a weak kicker, you fold. You *know* that the Rock has you beat. Against D-Bass, you should be more reluctant to fold the same hand since you know that there is a good chance he or she is out of line.

Similarly, when you find yourself with a good hand (top pair in hold 'em or 7-stud) then you should play it aggressively. Bet. He or she may raise with a lesser hand. Check-raise frequently. You know D-Bass has a betting reflex. You know that he or she will bet if you check, so set the trap and spring it. You can play your good hands aggressively against D-Bass.

You cannot easily bluff D-Bass. The old saying is, "never bluff a bluffer" and with D-Bass it holds true. He or she will tend to believe that you are bluffing. D-Bass thinks that you are a fancy play artist like he or she is. D-Bass will call with "something" just in case you are bluffing. D-Bass will see the flop or 4th and 5th street to see if he or she develops something. D-Bass is looking to put a play on you.

The Maniac

Maniacs bet and raise too much. Unlike D-Bass, Maniacs do not understand hand value, nor do they consider what you have. All they know is the power of unbridled aggression. They bet and raise with wild abandon hoping that you will fold or that they will stumble onto the best hand. If you ever get into a game in which there is a Maniac on a heater, it is a sight to behold. The whole table is likely to go on tilt. The Maniac, time and time again, starts with some rubbish hand that he or she bets and raises to the river. If the Maniac is on a heater, he or she will luck into more than his share of winners. He or she will have a mountain of chips and the rest of the table will be on tilt. You will see the steam rising off of the other players.

The main mistake Maniacs make is to bet and raise when they have no hope of a bluff being successful. Sometimes they have the best hand. Under those circumstances, their bets and raises are, of course, correct. Usually, however, they do not have the best hand – they have a draw (good or bad) and they are betting like it is the immortal nuts. In the latter case, if there is no hope of the opposition folding then the maniac is making a huge mistake.

Here is a list of mistakes that a Maniac typically makes. If you see a player making these mistakes then you may classify that player as a Maniac:

1. Betting reflex. The Maniac always bets if it is checked.

2. Frequent early raises with poor hands. Small pair are worth an unlimited number of raises on 3rd street in 7-Stud or pre-flop in hold 'em.

3. Plays top pair like it is the nuts – raise raise raise raise.

4. Frequently re-raises his drawing hands.

5. Frequently bluffs in situations in which he or she ought to *know* that the opponent is going to call.

The maniac may come from one of two schools of thought. Some Maniacs are crazy gamblers. They treat poker like it is roulette or craps. Gamble gamble gamble. They are not interested in winning small pots so they make sure that any pot they are in is large. They view poker as a pure function of luck. The *luckiest* player will win the day and if they are going to be the fortunate one then they want to win a lot. The other brand of Maniac are bluff addicts. If they perceive any chance of their opponent folding then they bet. Since they almost always perceive that their opponent might fold, they almost always bet or raise.

You will beat a Maniac by acquiring the best hand and manipulating the betting to your advantage. You can loosen up your requirements when dealing with maniacs. In fact, you probably should give his or her early raises almost no credit at all. You are looking to be dealt, or develop, a moderately strong hand. Remember: just because the Maniac frequently has nothing, it does not follow that he or she *always* has nothing. When up against maniacs you are in a *very* profitable situation. You are also in a very volatile situation. In the short term, luck will rule the day. Consider the following situation.

There are only two players, you and the maniac. The game is hold 'em. You each have $100. The Maniac proposes that you each bet a flat $50 per hand. There will be no other betting. Put up your $50 and deal the cards. The game will continue until one player has $200 and the other player has $0. In addition, the Maniac agrees to give you J-To and he or she will take a random hand. Do you want the bet? Will it help your decision to know that J-To is a 55% winner against a random hand? You have an edge. You should take the bet. It is possible, although *extremely* unlikely that neither of you will ever win the $200 since you could alternate winning hands forever. However, I am assured by poker writer and mathematician Brian Alspach that the results will almost certainly be that you will win the $200 60% of the time and the Maniac will win 40% of the time.

The example is meant to illustrate what playing against a maniac is like. You have an edge. He or she will give you an edge over and over, hand after hand. It will, however, not be cheap. Your draws will not be inexpensive. You are a massive favorite in the long run, but over the short haul, he or she could get lucky and beat you for a lot of chips. In fact, in the example, you will go broke 40% of the time.

Do not fold your marginal hands against maniacs. If you let them bluff you too frequently, you may take what is an incredible opportunity and turn it into a losing proposition. Get a hand and call them down. Induce bluffs and check-raise frequently. In short, let them beat themselves. Lastly, do not bluff maniacs. They are not capable of giving much thought to your hand, and they are apt to re-bluff, which is an excellent play against someone who is bluffing. Wait for a hand, even a marginal one.

The Fox

Foxes are the players that have put it all together. Foxes have a complete understanding of hand value and they know when their hand is likely the best. Moreover, they have a complete picture of *your* hand. They know the range of cards that you will play in each position. They know where they stand. The Fox also knows who can be bluffed and who cannot. In short, he or she knows when to zig and when to zag.

Beware the Fox. Every other player type has a particular mistake that he or she makes most commonly. The Fox has none. The Fox does not make unforced errors. He or she will make the occasional mistake. It is impossible to play a game like poker – a game of incomplete information – without making the occasional mistake. His error will not be brought on by lack of skill. It will be brought on by happenstance. Foxes are dangerous players who understand hand value. They read opponents well. They might hold almost anything when they enter a pot. At first glance, a Fox might appear to be an O-Tuna or a S-Fish, but he is not. Foxes *always* know where they are.

Here are some characteristics of the Fox. If you see these signs you may classify the player as a Fox:

1. He or she makes *large* adjustments based upon position (most player grossly underrate the importance of position – the Fox does not and he or she uses it as his battering ram).

2. Shifts gears. Foxes are not reliable. Sometimes he or she appears to be a Maniac and other times he or she appears to be a Rock.

3. Will raise and then fold in the same betting round when it is re-raised back to him.

The Fox is not thinking specifically about his hand. He or she is thinking about the other players in the pot, what hands they hold, pot odds, and the likelihood that he or she could succeed with a bluff. He or she is thinking about check-raising, position, tells, and slow playing. The Fox is playing the people not the cards. He or she has all the weapons in the poker arsenal and he or she uses them correctly.

You *cannot* win money from a Fox. They are the truly good players. By definition, you cannot win money in the long run from a player who is making a very high percentage of correct decisions. Do not try. Like it or not, your profit does not come from Foxes, even if you yourself are a Fox. A world class player. Your profit will come from poor players, not the other Foxes.

On the other hand, you cannot pick up your chips and quit just because one Fox has settled into your game (actually you can and sometimes should). You need to at least take away his advantage. You want the Fox to perceive you as a dangerous player who he or she has to reckon with. You must occasionally bluff. You must occasionally re-bluff. You must occasionally play your hand in an unexpected way. Predictable players get eaten alive by the Foxes. Beware: if you are too frequently out of line, the Fox will sense it.

You want Foxes on your right. They are very skilled at punishing the players whom they have position on and they fear players behind them. If you can get a seat move to get the Fox on your right, do so.

A Final Word on Player Types

O-Tuna and S-Fish are the most common providers in low-limit poker. Next are Rocks who are likely to be marginally profitable players in most low-limit games. D-Bass and Fox are fairly similar. In fact, in a lot of low-limit games D-Bass will be a profitable player. Despite making the frequent wrong move, their other skills are sufficient to see them through. Maniacs are not all that common. When you stumble onto one, fasten your seatbelt.

When you are at the table, assign each player a label. Say to yourself "The player in seat three is an O-Tuna." In addition, indicate if the player is *aggressive* or *timid*. Aggressive players will bet their draws. Their bets and raises do not necessarily reflect the strength of their hand. Timid players, on the other hand, are more predictable. Their bets are usually exactly in accordance with how strong they perceive their hand to be.

And one final note... the best situation is to *know* what *this* player has in *this* situation. Go beyond a simple classification and get to know each of your opponents intimately. Be a Fox. Concentrate on a player. Call up the past patterns you have seen from this player and act accordingly. In other words, do not stop thinking about a player once you have him in a box. Seek to better understand the limits of his particular box.

ADVANCED SKILLS

Deceptive Play

If you diligently play in accordance with the basic low-limit poker strategy (bet with the best – good draw to invest – fold all the rest), your betting pattern will be an exact reflection of the strength of your hand. Against little-skilled opponents, this will not matter. Little-skilled opponents are not paying attention. They will never realize that every time you bet, you have what you think is the best hand, and every time you just call, you have a good draw. Almost all of your profit comes from little-skilled opponents.

Just as you are classifying your opponents and studying their betting patterns, *some* of your opponents will be doing the same to you. *Some* of your opponents will be skilled. As you go up in level, more of your opponents will be skilled. A $10-20 game will, generally, have more skilled players than a $2-4 game. Skilled opponents will quickly realize that you are a Rock and play you accordingly. Skilled opponents will not give you any action. As you move up in level, it becomes more important to add deception to your game.

A word of warning: many novice and intermediate players over-value deception. An occasional deceptive play is all that is required to plant the seeds of doubt in your skilled opponent's mind. If you play deceptively too often, you risk becoming a maniac. When it comes to deceptive play, a little goes a long way.

Playing a hand deceptively means playing it *other than in accordance* with the basic low-limit poker strategy. It means betting or raising when you do *not* have the best hand, and calling or checking when you *do* have the best hand. Deceptive strategies must not be practiced randomly; they must be employed selectively. You must diverge from the basic low-limit poker strategy *only* when you have some compelling reasons for doing so.

Betting a Big Draw

If you have eight outs and two cards to come, it is 2-1 against you making your hand. If you have 8-7 and the flop in hold 'em is 9-6-2 , you have eight outs to the nuts (any ten or any five). The basic low-limit poker strategy calls for you to call with a good draw. If you follow this strategy, then you will check and call with your 8-7. Against one opponent, this is generally the correct strategy. Your expectation is that you will get back $1 out of every $3 that goes into the pot (2-1). Thus, against one opponent when you each put in $10 on the flop your expectation is that you will get back $6.66. You are losing on the money going into the pot, but the effective odds you are getting, because of the money already in the pot, make it a profitable play. In other words, you have a good draw. If you have two opponents and you each put in $10 then you expect to get back $10 (33% of $30). Against three opponents, you each put in $10 and you expect to get back $13.33. If you have three opponents, you can bet or raise with eight outs and you are making money on the money flowing into the pot. It is not only a good draw, it is a good bet.

Beware. It is not quite as simple as I just made it out to be. You are not guaranteed to win one out of three. Sometimes, one of your opponents will have the same hand as you, in which case you will improve to the nuts, but only win one half of the pot. Sometimes you will improve to a straight and one of your opponents will improve to a full house. Generally, however, big draws are an opportunity to add deception to your game at little or no long term cost. If you have eight outs *to the nuts* and at least three callers, you can bet or raise. You will probably increase your profits betting or raising against three callers. At worst, you have a *slight* negative expectation. Your long-term goal of deception will be served. You will be serving notice that you do not *only* bet or raise with the best hand. Note that you are betting against three *callers*, not opponents. If a player on your right bets, you raise, and the two players on your left fold, then you only have one caller. Namely, the original raiser. This play is available only if you are after three callers, or if you check-raise after there have been three callers.

If you have fifteen outs with two cards to come you are the favorite over even a single opponent. You can consider yourself to have the best hand. If you have 8♣-7♣, the flop is 9♣-6♣-2♥, and your opponents has A♠-9♦, then you are the favorite. You will win almost 57% of the time. If you have fifteen outs and two cards to come, you can bet or raise with impunity. You are not making money simply by calling with a good draw, you are making money on every dollar that your opponent puts into the pot on the flop. Again, beware. If you have a second opponent who has the nut flush draw, your fifteen outs are reduced to six (you need to complete a straight, but not the flush). Like eight outs and three opponents, you can bet or raise with 15 outs against one opponent and increase your profits. If you have less than fifteen outs, you will be in a marginally losing situation, but the cost will be offset by the deception that you have added to your game.

Principle: *With two cards to come and eight outs to the nuts, you may bet or raise against three callers. With two cards to come and fifteen outs, you may bet or raise against one caller. Generally, you will add deception without cost.*

It is important to note that you should *not* always be betting or raising your big draw. For example, suppose you hold 9♥-8♥ on the button. There are two limpers and so you, correctly, limp in. The small-blind also limps in, the big-blind checks and five of you see the flop of 2♥-6♣-7♥. You have flopped fifteen outs (any heart, any five, and any ten). It checks to the player immediately on your right who bets. You consider the above principle and you think to yourself "I have two cards to come with fifteen outs I should raise." If you raise in this case you may cause the first three players to fold. If you simply call then it is very likely in low-limit poker that one or more will call for the turn at least. You *probably* increase your profits in this case by inviting other players to call. The more the merrier. You have the best draw and if you make it you want to win as big a pot as possible. In this case, call.

Bluffing

Bluffing is betting or raising when you have a hand that is not the best. Your hope is that all of your opponents will fold and you will win the pot by default. Bluffing is a critical skill. If you *never* bluff then your skilled opponents will fold when you bet unless they have a better hand or a good draw. This does not mean that you should bluff indiscriminately. You should only bluff when it is profitable to do so.

155

Principle: *Only bluff when you have a* **reasonable** *chance of succeeding.*

If the pot is $100 and a bet will cost you $20, you only need to succeed one time out of five to win. Four times out of five you lose $20 for a total loss of $80, but one time out of five you succeed for a total win of $100. You are $20 ahead. "Reasonable" chance of success means that you will be profitable in the long run. Even still, many low-limit players bluff far too often. The profitability of your bluffs will depend upon how well you read your opponent. What is the chance that he or she will fold?

There are many factors to consider before launching a bluff. How many opponents are you facing? A bluff has a better chance of succeeding against one opponent than it does against many opponents. Particularly in low-limit poker, when the most common error of your opponents is calling too often, you will find it almost impossible to bluff three or more opponents. Limit your bluffs to hands in which you have only one or two opponents.

Bluff against opponents who have shown weakness. In 7-stud, if you are up against the bring-in bettor and he or she has checked to you on both 4th street and 5th street, go ahead and attempt a bluff. It is likely that his hand is weak. He or she started with a random hand (he or she was the bring-in) and checked to you twice. There is a good chance his hand is weak. This is a much better bluffing opportunity than bluffing against a player who raised you on 3rd street, and bet into you on 4th and 5th street. When you raise this player as a bluff, he or she is likely to actually have something – he or she has been betting, thus, showing strength.

> *"You won't believe this hand that I played against Crazy Eddie last night," Paul complained. "I raised before the flop with A-K. Everybody folds except for Crazy Eddie who is the big-blind. The flop is J-6-2 with no flush draw. Eddie checked so I bet."*
>
> *"And Eddie called?" I guessed.*
>
> *"Right! How did you know?"*

"It wouldn't be much of a story if he folded on the flop and you won the pot."

"Of course not." Paul continued, "Anyway the turn is a queen and Eddie checks again so I bet and he calls. Then the river is another queen and Eddie checks. I figure that he would have bet the turn if he had a queen so I bet again and Eddie calls with 3-2! He wins the pot with a lousy pair of deuces. What an idiot!"

"Yes you were," I nodded.

"Not me! Eddie! Eddie is the idiot."

"No." I shook my head, "You are the idiot. There was nothing much on the flop. Eddie is a screaming fish so when he called you on the flop, he could have had almost anything. But, when he calls you on the turn, he has something. The worst that he could have is ace high, which is the only thing that you can beat. You should have known that he was going to call you on the river. More importantly, on the river either you had the best hand or you were getting called and losing."

"But he called me all the way with a pair of deuces. Doesn't that make him an idiot?"

"If you had the best hand, he would look a fool. But, he beat you. You are the fool for bluffing in that situation."

This conversation with Paul illustrates two important points. First, "know your opponent." Crazy Eddie called the flop and the turn. It was very likely that Eddie was going to call the river as well. You must bluff selectively and only against players who *can* be bluffed.

Second, on the river when you have a hand that may be the best, generally you should not bet unless you will win if you are called. It is possible that Eddie has called all the way with an ace high. If he has, then Paul has the winning hand but Eddie will not call. If Paul checks, he wins the showdown; the same amount that he would have won by betting. On the other hand, if Paul gets called by a pair, he loses $20 that he need not have lost. Paul's bet is a losing proposition. If his A-K is the best hand, then he wins the pot. If it is not the best hand, he loses the pot. Betting on the river will not increase Paul's profit.

Bluff when you have outs. In *The Theory of Poker* Sklansky defines a "semi-bluff" as "a bet with a hand which you do not think is the best hand but which has a reasonable chance of improving to the best hand." In other words, bluff when you have a draw. This is not to suggest that you should routinely bluff when you have a draw. You cannot ignore the principle that you should only bluff when there is a reasonable chance of succeeding. If you are going to get called (or raised), betting your good draws will generally cost you money in the long run. It is preferable to semi-bluff (i.e. bluff when you have outs), but *it is still bluffing*. The general principle, therefore, that you should only bluff when you have a reasonable chance of succeeding still holds. You require *less* chance that your bluff will succeed since your diminished chance of success is offset by your chance of improving, but you still need *at least some* chance of success for a semi-bluff to be the right play.

Many low-limit players get overly enamored with semi-bluffing. They routinely bet or raise with flush draws and straight draws. You must not lose sight of the fact that a semi-bluff is still a bluff. If you know that you are going to be called then you should not bluff. Nor should you semi-bluff.

Slow Playing

Slow-playing is playing a hand weakly in an early betting round in order to increase your profits by betting or raising in a latter betting round. It is a deceptive play, since in an early betting round you will be checking or just calling with the best hand. You are sending your opponents the message that your checks and calls do not necessarily mean that you are weak. Sometimes you check and call with very powerful hands.

You should consider slow playing if your hand is very strong *and* it is likely that if you bet, all your opponents will fold. To take an extreme example, suppose in hold 'em you have A-A and the flop is A-A-2. You have a very strong hand. There is little danger of losing the hand by checking since it is extremely unlikely that any of your opponents will be able to develop a hand that can beat you. Your hope is that the turn card will give one of your opponents a hand strong enough to call you with. If a king appears on the turn, you might get called by a player with a hand like K-Q who would have folded on the flop had you bet. You must have a very strong hand to make slow playing correct. It is a terrible feeling to lose to a player who would have folded if you had bet.

In 7-stud, you can generally slow play when you start with three of a kind. It is the only time in 7-stud that you have a huge edge. In hold 'em, you can generally slow play anytime you flop a hidden three-of-a-kind (a pair in the hole matching one board card).

Check-raising

Check-raising is checking your hand and raising a player who bets on the same betting round. It is a deceptive play, since like slow playing, you are indicating that sometimes when you check, you will raise a bettor who has position on you. Your checks are not necessarily a sign of weakness. Sometimes when you check it is a sign of strength.

You should consider check-raising when you believe that you have the best hand and you are quite certain that a player behind you will bet if you check. It does you no good to check your hand intending to raise, only to discover that nobody behind you bets and you fail to spring your trap. Know your opponents. Will someone behind you bet if you check? Some players have a "betting reflex" and they automatically bet if they are in last position and it is checked to them. Maniacs and D-Bass often have a betting reflex.

In 7-stud, you can generally check-raise if you have a strong hand that is hidden. If your hand is not well hidden, it is more likely that your opponents will check behind you. If you have (A-7)-A-T and you check hoping to raise a player who is behind you, he will *know* that you have an ace-high at the very least. He is less likely to bet his moderate hands fearing that you have a pair of aces. If you have (A-A)-7-T, he his much more likely to bet if you check to him. In hold 'em, you can generally check-raise if you have the top pair on the flop with a good kicker.

Putting Your Opponents on a Hand: At the Start

Figuring out what your opponent has is a critical skill. Most low-limit players play according to some rote method. They always play K-Jo regardless of position or the number of bets; they never fold top pair no matter how many raises they must endure. You *might* be a winning player in this way, but the next skill to develop is the ability to fold big hands. If you never fold top pair, you are losing a lot of money that you need not lose.

The previous chapter gave you a player classification system. Classifying your opponent is the first step in putting him or her on a hand. Is the player in question a Rock? If so, you know he or she is holding "heavy" cards. If the player is an S-Fish then you know he or she could be holding almost anything. The second step in putting your opponent on a hand, is reconstructing the hand and asking yourself what the betting tells you about your opponent's holding.

Start by putting your opponents on a *range of hands* and then gradually narrowing the possibilities as the hand progresses. When you initially put a player on a hand you take into account what class of player he or she is, what the player's position is, and how he or she entered the pot. Rocks play a very narrow range of hands, S-Fish and Maniacs play a much wider range of hands. O-Tuna and D-Bass fall somewhere in the middle. Foxes will vary their range of hands according to position and game conditions.

As a player's position gets later and later, their range of playable hands generally increases. You will hear all sorts of players at low-limit games say, "I was in late position" or, "I was on the button." Even weak players have learned that they can play more hands in late position. Generally, however, they do not understand why this is. Weak players use late position as an *excuse* to call with hands that they should never consider playing. Nonetheless, you can put players on an increasingly wide range of hands as their position gets later.

How did this player enter the pot? Did he or she limp in or did this player call one or two raises? If he or she limped in, was he the first limper or was there a series of limpers in the pot first? Generally, players will tighten up when there has been a raise. Even S-Fish and O-Tuna will ditch their worst hands when facing a raise. Similarly, after there have been several limpers, players will limp in with more and more hands. If there have been three limpers, you can expect to see more, since the players will smell a big pot in the offing and want to take their shot at it.

Did this player raise? Did he or she put in the first, second, or third raise? Generally, when a player raises you can narrow his or her range of hands. S-Fish and O-Tuna may not have a good grasp on hand value, but if either one is raising then he or she *thinks* the hand is worth raising.

The following table lists various factors and how they effect any given player classification's range of starting hands. To use the table, cross reference the event on the left with the player type across the top. You will find a "range of hands" listed as tiny, small, medium, large, or huge.

Event	S-Fish	O-Tuna	Maniac	Rock	D-Bass	Fox
Limp in Early	Large	Medium	Large	Small	Medium	Small
Limp in Middle	Large	Large	Large	Medium	Large	Medium
Limp in Late	Huge	Large	Large	Large	Large	Large
Raises Early	Medium	Small	Large	Tiny	Large	Tiny
Raises Late	Medium	Medium	Huge	Small	Large	Large
Calls a Raise	Large	Medium	Large	Small	Medium	Small
Many Limpers	Huge	Huge	Huge	Large	Huge	Huge

I have not defined the hand ranges specifically. The table is simply meant to illustrate how you should adjust the range of hands that you are putting a player on according to how he or she initially enters a pot. You can give each "hand range" a specific definition, although I do not recommend being that rigid. It is easier in hold 'em to give each hand range a specific guide. As an example, you could assume the hand ranges to approximate the following:

Tiny: Big pairs and big aces.

Small: Big pairs, big aces, medium pairs, and K-Q.

Medium: Big pairs, big aces, medium pairs, random big cards, and suited aces.

Large: Big pairs, big aces, medium pairs, small pairs, random big cards, suited aces, suited kings, suited queens, and suited connectors.

Huge: Any two cards.

For example, a Rock in early position is the first player to enter the pot and he or she does so by raising. What has the Rock got? You can be sure that he or she has a small range of hands. For that reason, you would never consider calling a Rock's raise unless you have a very strong hand, or unless there are a lot of other callers in front of you and you can expect to win a huge pot if you make your draw.

Putting Your Opponents on a Hand: As the Hand Develops

After more cards have been dealt – the flop in hold 'em or 4th street in 7-stud – you will have more information and you can further narrow down the range of hands that your opponent may have. If a player bets then he or she is representing some strength; if a player raises he or she is representing more strength. Similarly, if a player checks he or she represents weakness; if a player calls he or she represents a drawing hand. A player could be playing deceptively, but for the most part you should take players' checks, bets, and raises at face value.

The game is 7-stud. You are the forced bring-in with (7♣-7♦)-4♦. You are called by an O-Tuna two seats to your left with (X-X) 9♣, and by a Rock on his left with (X-X)-8♦. What are you putting your two opponents on? The O-Tuna will have a large range of hands. He or she could have a three-flush, a three-straight, a small pair in the hole, a pair of nines, or any variety of hands that he or she considers adequate starters in 7-stud. What about the Rock? He or she will have a medium range of hands. The Rock did not raise, so it is likely that he or she hopes to develop the hand at a minimum cost.

On the fourth street you hold (7♣-7♦)-4♦-T♣, the O-Tuna has (X-X)-9♣-J♥, and the Rock has (X-X)-9♣-2♣. The O-tuna is first to act and bets. What does he or she have? The O-Tuna had a large range of hands on third street that were only worth a call, but now on 4th street with the addition of the J♥ the O-Tuna is betting. You should assume that the jack has improved his or her hand. Did he or she start with a straight draw that got better? What about a straight draw that included a jack and now he or she has a pair of jacks? In any event, you should probably assume that the O-Tuna has, at the minimum, a small pair that he or she feels is the best hand, or a big straight draw. The Rock calls. What does he or she have? The Rock is still not raising and yet he or she still likes the hand enough to continue putting money into the pot. Put the Rock on a medium pair or a four flush.

As the hand progresses to 5th street and beyond, you can further narrow the possible range of hands. If the Rock lands the 4♣ on 5th street and starts raising you can bet that he or she has made a flush. Play your hand accordingly. Once you *know* what your opponents have, you will know how to play your hand.

Accurately putting your opponents on hands is a critical skill. You must practice it. Furthermore, you must learn to trust yourself because you want to learn to fold losing hands and extract extra money from your opponents with winning hands. Fortunately, this skill is easy to practice. The next time you play, do it every hand. Not only the hands that you are involved in, but the hands you have folded as well. Put players on ranges of hands, narrow the range as the hand progresses, and call their hand exactly at the showdown. Particularly against little-skilled low-limit opponents, you will find that you will become remarkably able to predict your opponents' hands. When you are able to do this, and have faith in your ability, you will be able to save a lot of money by folding hands that other players never dream of releasing.

Discipline

It is no good to know what you *ought* to do unless you actually *do it*. Boredom is the enemy of discipline. Some nights you will sit and sit and sit. Hand after hand you will find cards that do not fit the starting hand guide. When you have these nights you will be tempted to wade into the fray with lesser hands. In hold 'em J-7s will start to look good. In 7-stud (A-K)-9 will start to look good. Good poker players not only know what to do, but also have the discipline to do it consistently. As Mike Caro would say, "Play your best game *all the time*."

As a simple example, suppose you only ever entered the fray with the best hand. In a ten handed hold 'em game, you will enter the fray only 10% of the time. This alone can be boring. When you suffer a long streak of poor cards, the boredom demon will really work his magic on you. This is when you will need discipline. Tell yourself that even though right now you are in the middle of a streak of poor cards, sometime in the future you will enjoy a streak of good cards. There are feasts and there are famines. When you are in the midst of a famine, you will risk losing your discipline. If you lose discipline, you risk losing so much money that you will not be able to make up for your loss when the feast arrives.

Take a handful of pebbles and throw them on the ground. You know that their distribution is random because you threw them and yet, they will *appear* to have a pattern. Some of the pebbles will group together in little clusters. So it is with the hands that you are dealt. At times, it will *appear* that there is pattern. It will appear that you are getting a cluster of bad cards. You are. Relax. Sooner or later you will get a cluster of good cards. You must maintain discipline.

CHAPTER EIGHT

TELLS

A "tell" is something that a player does or says, either consciously or unconsciously, that gives a hint as to the quality of his hand. It is something that your opponent does or says that "tells" you what he or she has. According to Hollywood, a tell is often as specific as *listening* to an Oreo cookie break when one is bluffing and *watching* the cookie break when one has a real hand (ever see the movie *Rounders* with Matt Damon and Ed Norton?). There are players who exhibit such specific tells, but most tells you see are general in nature. Most tells you see can be categorized and you will see the categories time and time again.

Once you start looking, you will be surprised to discover how much information your little-skilled, low-limit opponents are giving away. There is a mountain of information available at the poker table – particularly in games populated by weak opposition. Your job is to start looking for it.

No section on tells would be complete without mentioning Mike Caro's *Book of Tells: The Body Language of Poker*. This book is filled with photos and examples of a whole variety of tells. I have picked out five tells that I consider particularly common and useful at low-limits. Additionally, you can study any number of psychology texts that deal with body language. You will find them useful, but not nearly as useful and applicable to poker as Mr. Caro's work.

Read this book. Then, start taking notes. When studying your opponents you are looking for both general trends and specific quirks. Also remember that tells are never the whole story. They are another piece of the puzzle. Classify your opponent, analyze his betting pattern, and look for tells. Use all of your tools to put your opponent on a hand and play accordingly.

Hang on, hang on ... I need a second to think

In Caro's *Book of Tells* he titles this, 'Let Me Think Awhile' and he describes it this way: "Players will seldom delay limit poker games by taking an extra-long time to make a decision. When [a player] leans back and considers his situation, it's probably a borderline decision."

When players have to stop and think about whether to call, fold, or raise, they are not making *for them* a routine decision. Whatever their hole cards, their choice of action is not obvious and they want to think about it. This means that as soon as you see one of your opponents pause to think, you can probably rule out a whole variety of holdings on his part. You cannot be certain what the player has, but you can be certain what he or she does *not* have. You opponent does not have a hand that, *for him or her*, is a routine decision. In little-skilled low-limit games, your opponent almost certainly does *not* have: (1) top pair in hold 'em; (2) two pair in 7-stud; (3) a four-card Flush; or (4) an open ended Straight draw. Rare is the low-limit player who will fold any of those hands. If he or she really has to think about it, then you can rule out those possibilities.

If you see a player think for a long time, your job is to figure out *what* the player is thinking about.

Let me give you a specific example of how you might use this tell. It is $10-20 hold 'em. You are the big-blind and you hold A-9o. There are two callers and the little blind calls so there are four of you that see the flop of A-8-7 of different suits. You have flopped top pair with a 9 kicker. Not bad, but not great. You bet. Ernie the S-Fish calls without hesitation. All the other players fold so it is now heads up, you versus Ernie.

You know this S-Fish well. You have played with Ernie any times. He is generally a loose and passive player. Ernie will not raise without a big hand and he will call all the way to the river with just about anything. Ernie the S-Fish is the kind of opponent you dream about. He is also the kind of opponent that is not uncommon in little-skilled low-limit games. Ernie's call of your bet on the flop does not narrow his hand down too much – he could have anything from top pair to a double gut-shot backdoor straight draw. The turn card is a jack. You still have top pair and a weak kicker. You bet. Ernie takes a long pause: "Hang on, hang on... I need a second to think."

As soon as he has to stop and think about calling, you learn a lot about his hand. In the first place, this S-Fish is a predictable player, which is important since it makes figuring him out easier. On the flop S-Fish had (for him) a routine call. This does not tell you much since almost any two cards qualify as a routine call on the flop. On the turn, the jack caused him to stop and think. If the jack helped him, it is not likely to have helped him very much. Ernie is not holding T-9 for a straight. If he had a routine call on the flop and then the jack improved his hand he would surely have a routine call on the turn. Ernie does not. He has to think about it. Thus, the jack either did not improve him or improved him only very slightly. Also – and this is the more important part – Ernie the S-Fish does not have an ace! You have him beat! There is no doubt that if he did hold an ace (top pair), he would call without hesitation. Calling with top pair is a routine play. It does not require any thought.

The river card is another jack. Perfect. You bet. If the jack on the turn was no help, then neither was the jack on the river. You are sure that Ernie does not hold an ace. Without his tell on the turn, you might be forced to check and call the river fearing that he has an ace with a kicker bigger than your 9. But, you know he or she does not have an ace so, you bet. S-Fish calls. You turn over your hand and he throws his into the muck. Another $20 in your stack that you would not otherwise get, except for the tell on the turn.

What do you do to ensure that you do not give this tell to your opponents? Obviously, you must occasionally take time to make a routine decision. Do not *automatically* call when holding top pair medium kicker. You must occasionally pause before calling but be careful. You will find that in low-limit games, the players will become annoyed if you constantly take a long time to act on your hand. You must, however, vary the speed of your play so that when you need time to think it will not give off this tell to your observant opponents.

A Wind-sucking, Knee-pumping, Wing-ding of a Good Time

In Caro's *Book of Tells*, he titles this tell "It's Exciting to come out fighting!" and he describes it this way: "The shaking is uncontrollable. Remember it's a release of tension, not fear, that makes this player shake as he bets."

When stressed, the human animal responds physiologically. Specifically, you probably experience an immediate jump in heart and respiratory rate when faced with a sudden confrontation. Also, your quick twitch muscles will tighten and ready for action. What you are experiencing is natural and evolutionary. What you are experiencing can also be a dead giveaway at the poker table.

In a poker game, most hands are routine. You look at your cards, they are poor and you fold. Suddenly you look down and see Q-Js. You attempt a steal raise on the button. The big-blind calls. The flop is T-9-4. You have a straight draw. Your opponent checks. You bet hoping that the big-blind will now fold, but he or she calls. The turn is a complete miss. Its a 4. Your opponent checks and you check. Suddenly the river pops up a dream king. You have the nuts. Your opponent bets. You raise! You are having a wind-sucking, knee-pumping, wing-ding of a good time.

As the hand progressed you were placed under increasing tension. Your pre-flop raise was called and then your flop bluff was called and then you missed your draw on the turn and then you hit the nuts on the river. That, in Mike Caro's words, is a release of tension. I can *guarantee* that you will be experiencing some physiological changes over the course of the hand. Specifically, you will experience an increase in heart and respiratory rate. And you will get "twitchy."

This tell is particularly obvious when playing against players who are new to the game. They have not yet experienced hitting the nuts on the river enough times to dull themselves to it. New players will, therefore, tend to suffer more extreme physiological consequences.

What should you look for? The most obvious thing is a jump in respiratory rate. You see it frequently. You will see it more pronounced in people who are overweight. In a nutshell, when you see a player suddenly start to suck wind, you know that some significant outside force is suddenly acting upon his or her physiology. The key is spotting the precise moment at which the wind sucking begins. In hold 'em, if your opponent starts to suck wind as soon as he or she sees his pocket cards, your opponent *likes* what he or she sees. Aces or kings? If he or she was looking at a hand like 9-5o then it would be a routine fold and not cause any stress. If your opponent starts sucking wind as soon as the flop hits then he or she *likes* the flop. Did your opponent flop a set? Top pair big kicker?

This tell can also giveaway a bluff. If your opponent is just sitting there like a bump on a log, you check, and he or she bets – pauses – and then sucks wind your opponent might be bluffing. It is possible that he or she missed the flop (no stress), you checked (no stress), and then he or she decided to bluff. At first your opponent will be acutely aware of their physiology. He or she will stop breathing and sit perfectly still. As you sit staring at your opponent the stress will build and build and the heart rate and breathing will increase. If there is a long pause, followed by wind sucking you may have identified a bluff.

This tell is a better way to pick off a player who likes his hand, but it can be used to spot a bluff *occasionally*. The key thing to make note of is the *moment* at which the stress manifests itself. Then ask yourself, what is causing the stress?

Most often you will notice breathing, but knee pumping is also quite common. If a player who normally sits calmly suddenly starts pumping his knee under the table on the flop, you know that an outside force has acted upon his physiology. Translation: he likes the flop. You will also see an involuntary shrug from players that like the flop. Their quick twitch muscles fire as soon as they get that adrenaline hit. It is subtle; but some players do it *every single time* that they like the flop.

In the first major no-limit hold 'em tournament I won, I remember watching a hand in which two players saw the flop. They both looked at the board. One of them started to suck wind and the other one started to pump his knee. I thought to myself, "One of these two is going to lose their stack this hand." They both checked the flop. On the turn wind-sucker shoved his whole stack in and knee-pumper called. Wind-sucker flopped two pair and knee-pumper flopped a set which stood up. Wind-sucker was eliminated.

What do you do to ensure that you do not give this tell to your opponents? The first thing you need is experience. The more hands of poker you play, the more things become routine. The higher the limits you play, the less the stress will effect you. If I ever get to the final table of the World Series of Poker Championship, I am pretty sure that I am going to suck a lot of wind because the prospect of a $2,500,000 payday will act on me in new and unusual ways. So, even experience will not solve all the situations in which you will (hopefully) find yourself. The other thing I suggest is playing each hand in the same manner. Play with a rhythm. Look at your cards (beat) bet (beat) look at the flop (beat) concentrate on breathing (beat). In other words, if you fear that your experience at this level will cause unusual stress, or that your opponents are particularly observant, get into a routine and stick to it. Routine will tend, physiologically, to make your heart and respiratory rate more manageable.

How Big is My Flush Draw?

In Mike *Caro's Book of Tells* he calls this "One of my cards was red?" and he describes it this way: "Players remember denominations more readily than they do suits... For this reason, if the flop is suited, players must look back to see if they have a card of that suit."

I consider this to be one of *the* most reliable low-limit tells. In hold 'em, once a third suited card hits the board, and in 7-stud once a player gets two or three suited board cards, if your opponent takes another peek at his hole cards, he or she is looking to see if *one* of them is suited to the cards you can see. For instance, if the flop is all clubs and a player takes another peek at his or her hole cards you can bet that he or she does *not* have a flush. If he or she had two clubs in his pocket you might expect to see him start to suck wind, but he or she would have no need to double check since if his pocket cards are suited he or she will remember that much. The player in question does not have a flush. He has offsuit cards and he or she is wondering if one of them is a club. You can bet top pair with impunity.

In 7-stud, a player will often peek at his hole cards if his up cards are the same suit. You can be sure that he or she does *not* have four cards of the same suit. If he or she started with three clubs and 4th street was another club, he or she does not need to look back at his hand. On the other hand, if he or she starts with a pair and 4th street shows two suited cards, he or she may think to himself, "Hey, I might be backing into a flush. I better check the suit of the cards in my pocket." If he or she gets another suited card on 5th street, you know he or she does not have a flush... yet. Similarly, in 7-stud if an opponent gets three suited cards face up on 5th or 6th and he or she double checks the hole cards then you know that he or she does not yet have a flush. You opponent is checking to see if he or she had a fourth suited card in the hole.

What will this tell do for you? There is an obvious advantage in knowing that your opponent does not yet have a flush. On the current street, you can bet your hand for value. On a future street in either hold 'em or 7-stud, if he or she gets another flush card you know there is a good chance that he or she has made his flush and you should consider folding.

What should you be doing to keep from giving this tell to your opponents? Obviously you should be committing your hole cards to memory. Avoid the necessity of looking back at your pocket to see if one of your A-K was a club or not. Memorize them. I do not think that there is any special tip that I can give you that will help you. I recite my cards in my head by rank from highest to lowest and then the suits in the same order. If I have A♣-K♥ in the hole, I say to myself "Ace-King clubs and hearts." It works for me. Whatever you do, you will need to commit them to memory. It is not hard. The only reason that people do not commit their cards to memory is that they are unaware of the importance of not peeking back at their hole cards!

A second word of warning. Some players are peekers. Some players look back at their hole cards frequently. Almost compulsively. They peek at their hole cards on every street. Or, they peek at their hole cards randomly and for no apparent reason at all. Whatever the reason, a small minority of low-limit players peek back at their cards a lot. It is not hard to identify which players at the table do this, but it is critical that you identify them lest you think they are peeking to see if they have another suited card when in fact they are looking back to admire the flush they have just completed.

Paul suddenly got what could only be described as a fox-like grin. "Do you ever use reverse tells? You know, to pretend you have something that you don't?"

"You can," I agreed. "You need to be certain that you are showing your reverse tell to a player who is capable of understanding what he is seeing."

"So you would only use reverse tells against skilled opponents?"

"Exactly. But not only do you need skilled opponents, they have to think that you are a little-skilled player," I cautioned. "If a Fox thinks that you are a Fox, he is not going to pay much mind to your apparent tell because he knows that it might be a put on."

"But if a Fox thinks I am a Screaming Fish then he might buy my little act?"

"Exactly," I smiled. "At advanced levels of poker you must not only categorize your opponents, you must understand how they have categorized you."

"It seems that as the skill level goes up, the cards matter less?"

"Paul," I smiled, "I think you are going to get this game figured out."

A Bet with a Story

In Mike Caro's *Book of Tells* he calls this "Ah, what's the difference? I bet" and he describes it this way: "[A Player] accompanying his bet with a shrug."

I like to call this tell "a bet with a story" which is what was often said by the first inveterate Rock I ever met. If ever someone called or bet or raised with a shrug or a comment, Chuck would always say "a bet with a story." Chuck had noticed what Mike Caro teaches. Namely, that players will usually act in the way opposite of the truth. If they have a very strong hand, they will act weak and if they have a weak hand they will act strong. In my experience, this phenomenon is most obvious when a player is holding a strong hand.

In particular, be wary of "a bet with a story." A player might, for instance, make a bet while shrugging. He or she might actually say "I guess

175

I will bet." A player might let out a loud sigh while pushing the chips forward. There are any number of things that he or she might do that will indicate uncertainty about this very treacherous bet. He or she is, in fact, not uncertain at all. Your opponent likes his or her hand and is pretending to be tentative. Players will often, either consciously or not, act in a way opposite to the truth.

For instance, in my regular game, John will *always* fire his chips into the pot if he is bluffing or has a weak hand, and will take a long time before slowly slipping his chips into the pot with a strong hand. It took me a long time to notice this tell because the difference is actually more subtle than that. It is not really "fire" versus "slip." It is more like the difference between a confident bet and a slightly hesitant bet. The difference is actually quite subtle, but it is there in John's case 100% of the time. This falls into the category of "a bet with a story." John's "story" is that he is tentative when he is actually confident.

This tell can be viewed as conscious or subconscious. Conscious tells are extroverted and obvious. The big shrug with a bet for instance. Subconscious tells are much more subtle. The players in question may not even be aware that you are observing, but they are putting on a behavior hoping that you notice their subtlety and try and take advantage of the situation.

To keep from giving this tell, like others, you must become a player of routine. I know a professional middle limit player from the Toronto area who has a set routine. He waits for the action to get to him. He looks at his cards by pulling up two corners. He looks at the cards while he counts to five in his head. He then folds or replaces his cards and announces his action in a clear voice: "I call." He then makes his bet with his right hand and stacks the chips in the pot the very same way. He finishes by staring at the pot. Same routine every hand whether he or she has A-A or 3-2.

In hold 'em, I do not look at my cards until the action reaches me. Then, before I look at my cards, I make my decision. For instance, I might decide that I am going to call with any "late position" cards, raise with any big pair or big ace, and fold all the rest. When I look at my hole cards, I can act almost instantly. In 7-stud, I prefer to look at my hole cards immediately since I am not so good at remembering all of the up cards that I have seen. By looking at my hole cards, I am able to concentrate on remembering cards that are relevant to my hand. After looking at my hole cards and glancing at my opponents' door cards, I will immediately formulate my 3rd street plan. When the action reaches me, I will be able to act very quickly. Make sure that you make the same betting motion each and every betting round.

I am Getting Ready to Call You

In Mike Caro's *Book of Tells* he creates "Caro's Law of Tells #15: Players reaching for their chips out of turn are usually weak."

Mr Caro's point is that players who know that they are being watched are often behaving opposite to their actual desire. If a player has reached

for his chips out of turn, as if he or she is going to bet or call, and this player knows that you are watching, you have to ask yourself, "Why is he or she doing that?" There is a good chance this player is attempting to talk you into something. Since this player is attempting to demonstrate that there is no chance of you winning with a bluff, you can assume that he or she is attempting to talk you out of bluffing. Maybe you should attempt it.

However, there is a codicil: "Players reaching for their chips out of turn are *consistent*." If you notice that Audrey reaching for her chips means that she does not want you to bet then you can be almost certain that she will be consistent with that move. On the other hand, you might notice that when George reaches for his chips he invariably calls your bet. He too will be consistent.

Some players reach for their chips as a ploy. Other players reach for their chips to hurry along the inevitable. They think they are beat, but they have to call you because they have a hand that fits into their definition of "hands that cannot be folded." For instance, there are a lot of low-limit players that will *never* fold top pair. They will dramatically throw their chips into the pot and then show their hand to their neighbor on the river when they are shown what they already know – they were beat all along. They show their cards to their neighbor as if to say, "You see, I had to call. I had top pair and it is just my bad luck that I was beaten again."

Your job is to figure out whether this particular player is attempting to convince you to bet, or not, by some physical action, or whether he or she is hurrying the inevitable. They might even say something. Players generally are consistent. If you notice that their "move" one occasion means that you should call, it will mean that on all occasions. You must learn what each player's particular predilection is. If you know nothing about the player, assume he or she is hoping you will believe his act. You therefore should do the opposite.

CHAPTER NINE

TRACKING YOUR RESULTS

The Critical Skill of Keeping Track

This chapter is critical. Maybe *the most critical in the* book. The message of this chapter is *very* simple. You must start keeping track of all your poker results. Not next week, or next month, or next year. You must start keeping track immediately.

Tonight, when you go to the casino or card room, write down the following: (1) what you played – game and limit; (2) how long you played – rounded off to the nearest quarter-hour; and (3) how much you won or lost – net, not gross. Start tonight. Do it every single time you play poker. It does not matter whether the game is in a casino, card room, or dorm-room. It does not matter if the game is for $0.25 or for $1000. It does not matter if the game is hold 'em or crazy-pineapple-with-a-pitch. Keep track! Do it starting tonight.

You will discover that you are a winner, a loser, or a liar. Ask around at your local card room or casino. How many of the regulars consider themselves winning poker players? My educated guess is that 80% of card room and casino poker players will tell you that they are winners at the end of the year. The other 20% will tell you that they do it for recreation, and that they more-or-less break even at the end of the year. The truth is, at least 90% of casino or card room poker players are losers. Why? There is a rake. The house takes something like 10% of the pot to a maximum of $3 each and every hand. This means for every hour of play, the house makes about $120. That's a lot of money coming out of the game.

There is no way most casino or card room players are winners. *No way.* To be a winner, you must not only be a better player than your opponents, but also be better by a margin sufficient to overcome the rake! Start keeping track and you will know if you are a winner or a loser. You will not be able to lie to yourself. You will not be able to fool yourself. You will discover that you are a winner, a loser, or a liar. As a side note, keep track of all gambling: bingo, sports betting, lottery tickets, blackjack, slots, etc. You may be surprised by what you discover.

Keep track and you will learn to love losing. Poker is a game of skill. If there is any doubt in your mind about this, skip directly to bingo and lottery tickets and forget about poker. Sorry to have wasted your time. Poker is a game of skill. Believe it. In the long run, the most skillful players will make money. In fact, if the game went on forever, the single most skillful player would get *all* the money.

In the long run the best player wins. But, in the short run it is luck that determines the winner. For example, suppose I were to play one hand of no-limit hold 'em against Doyle Brunson (the most famous and possibly the best no-limit hold 'em player in history). Suppose also that Doyle and I agreed to put all of our money in without looking at our cards. If I could get Doyle to agree (I couldn't) then it would be a 50/50 shot. A coin flip. Now suppose that instead of just shoving in our money, Doyle and I *played* 100 hands, or 1000 hands. With each hand, Doyle and I face decisions: bet, raise, fold, or call. For every single decision that I am wrong and Doyle is right, his chance of winning my money increases. Suddenly, it's not a coin flip. Suddenly, it's "Doyle gets rich and I go home broke... guaranteed."

The point is, in the short run you will either win or lose. In the long run (if you are Doyle), you will win. Track all of your results and you will come to see that in the short-term it is luck, but in the long run is it skill. Then, when a horrible player goes runner-runner straight flush to two perfect cards to beat your flopped four of a kind (989-1 by the way), you will be able to shrug your shoulders and say: "Whatever will be, will be." In other words, if you have proven to yourself that you are a winning player in the long run, short term losses will not bother you because all they mean is that the bad player got lucky – *this time.* You will learn to love losing. If you never lost, there would be no fish in the sea.

Keep track of all your results and you will learn that nothing happens quickly. When you are at a table with Loudmouth Larry who is constantly berating the other players, ask Larry one question: "How much money do you make per hour playing poker?" If Larry is actually a winning player, and he actually keeps track of all his wins and losses then he will know the answer. More often than not, the Loudmouth Larrys do not know the answer and they reveal themselves to be what you suspected all along – schmucks.

The truth is, it is almost impossible to win more than two big bets per hour at a casino or card room poker game. In a 3-6 hold 'em game, the maximum you can win is around $12/hour. In the short term, it will be a lot more or a lot less (that is the effect of luck). In the long term, however, it will be about $12/hour. Good players do not win every hand. Bad players win lots of hands. At the end of the year, you will find that you make about $12/hour in a 3-6 hold 'em game. Thus to *expect* to win $10,000 playing $3-6 hold 'em, you should count on playing for 833 hours or the equivalent of over twenty weeks working at a fulltime job. In actual fact, two big bets per hour is *very* hard to maintain over the long haul. It is much more likely to expect one big-bet per hour, which means that $10,000 is now 1666 hours away. At forty hours per week, that's 40 weeks. Playing $3-6 hold 'em as though it is a fulltime job it will take you almost a year to win just $10,000. That's why there are no professional $3-6 players. You can't make enough money to support yourself.

Nothing happens fast even though, at times, it seems to. You make or lose $400 in a single evening of $3-6 hold 'em and you feel like you are Doyle Brunson. Start tracking all of your results and you will see that you are a skillful player who got damn lucky over *that* short term period. In the long run, you will make between $6 and $12 per hour in that game. In other words, accumulating money playing poker takes time. It's not NASCAR. Nothing happens quickly. Be patient.

I can think of no single, simple thing that you can do *starting today* that will be of greater long term help than that. Start keeping track. Keep keeping track.

Principle: *Keeping track of every single cent you win and lose is not important – it is* **essential.** *You will discover that you are a winner, loser, or liar. You will learn to laugh at defeat and bask in victory.*

Your Poker Bankroll

Related to keeping track of your wins and losses is the maintenance of your bankroll; which is the amount of money you have set aside that is "poker money." If you are a professional player, it is critical to maintain a bankroll large enough to make a living without fear of going broke.

Like the stock market, your poker bankroll will tend to move up and down. Overall, however, it will move up if you are a winning player. A common analogy in the world of the stock market is that of a man walking his dog on a long leash. The man walks through a park in a straight line. He follows the sidewalk. The dog, on other hand, will run back and forth, hither and yon. They will both wind up at the other side of the park. Think of the man as your growing poker bankroll. Slowly but surely, he makes his way across the park; slowly but surely, your poker bankroll grows. The dog is your individual poker sessions or even individual hands. It will skip and hop in various directions and there is no way, in the short run, to predict where it will go next. Overall, however, it is headed to the far side of the park.

If you are a professional player, you will need to have a bankroll sufficient to withstand the standard deviation of the dog. You will need to have deep enough pockets to weather the storm and *the storm is coming*. There will *always* be a storm in your poker future. No matter how good you are, you will eventually hit a losing skid. For a thorough and insightful discussion of "How Much Do You Need?" see Mason Malmuth's *Gambling Theory and Other Topics*. Mr Malmuth is thorough and correct.

If you are an amateur player, you do not need to worry about losing your poker bankroll. From your next paycheck, take some of that money and go play! You can do this, but let me give you some advice. Build and maintain a poker bankroll separate from your day to day money. Unlike the pro, you need not worry about losing your poker bankroll because your next paycheck from the bakery, or the radio station, or the doctor's office, will cover your rent. However, having a separate poker bankroll will do a couple of things for you.

It will help you to keep track. If you have ignored the advice of a moment ago and you are not religiously keeping track of your wins and losses, having a separate bankroll will force you to keep track. If you started the year with $1000 in your bankroll and you find yourself with $2000 in the middle of March, you know that you have been a winner for those 2 ½ months. You are *de facto* keeping track even without writing it all down. Similarly, if you find that you are never able to get a separate bankroll started, it should be obvious to you that you are *not* a winning player.

I keep enough money in my poker bankroll to pay airfare, accommodation, and entry into the World Series of Poker Championship ($10,000), plus have enough left over that I can keep playing poker after I am the first to bust out of the tournament. If I get more money than that in my bankroll, I save it for retirement or buy an expensive gift for my wife. Both of these things increase the chance that I will be permitted to one day go and play the World Series of Poker Championship.

This leads me to the second reason for an amateur poker bankroll – honesty. My experience is that everyone, yourself included, will feel a lot better about your hobby if you keep it separate from your family finances.

This will, I admit, result is some odd conversations with friends and family. The first "major" poker tournament I won paid $9,040. My wife asked me: "What are we going to do with the money?" My boss asked me: "What are you going to do with the money?" My father asked me: "What are you going to do with the money?" My answer to each was the same: "I am going to use it to play poker. It is not money to me. To me, it is poker chips." They were, of course, freaked out.

Look at it this way. Suppose my hobby is making toy soldier nut crackers on a wood lathe. I am pretty good at it. In fact, last year I made $9,040 selling nutcrackers at the local hobby show. Nobody would look at me twice if I told them, "I am going to use that money to buy a better lathe so that I can make even better nut crackers." So it is with your amateur poker bankroll. You need to save a lot of money to play at higher and higher levels. And, to enjoy all that the hobby has to offer, you want to pursue that dream. Making a final table at the World Series of Poker is a pretty good feeling. So start saving for a wood lathe.

As a rule of thumb, you will need 300 times the big bet to have a safe poker bankroll. If you are a winning player and you only play $3-6, maintain a poker bankroll of $1800. If you fancy yourself to be a $15-30 player, you will want at least $9000 to feel comfortable. Most amatuer poker players (and most pros) overplay their bankrolls.

Principle: *Professional players require a bankroll that is large enough to cover their living expenses and the inevitable losing streak that is coming. Amateur players should have a separate bankroll because it makes life easier.*

CHAPTER TEN

HOME GAMES

M any people are introduced to poker at a "home game" where there is no house taking a rake, but rather a group of friends get together and play poker. Home games are generally social events as much as they are gambling events. Casino poker is fairly standardized the world over. There are some differences from casino to casino and country to country. Overall, casino poker is more the same than it is different. Home games... not so much.

Despite popular opinion, poker is not illegal in most jurisdictions. There is nothing wrong with getting together with your friends to play poker. There is nothing wrong with betting on the outcome of the hand. Just like there is nothing illegal about making a bet with your brother on the outcome of a football game, there is nothing illegal about betting with your brother on the outcome of a game of cards. The problem arises when somebody takes a rake. At this point, you cease to be a friendly poker game and become a "gaming house." It is at this point that the government wants to know what is going on so that they can regulate things and get their piece of the action. Think of the government as the house's house.

Also despite popular opinion, you cannot escape the illegality of running a raked game by claiming that "it wasn't a rake, it was a voluntary donation." The game is either raked or not. Judges are not stupid people. They will neither be fooled nor sympathetic towards the obvious fiction of a "donation."

I am not particularly opposed to raked home games. I figure that if a bunch of guys want to get together and pay Paul a rake in exchange for using his facilities for a poker game, this is an arrangement between those guys and Paul. On the other hand, if I am going to play in a raked game, I prefer to play in a public casino or card room because then I have recourse if I am unjustly treated. If, for instance, the house refused to cash my chips in a raked home game, there is not much I can do. On the other hand, if a public casino refuses to cash my chips, I do have some recourse through the managing government agency or the courts.

For the sake of this list, "home game" means a poker game that is held at a "private" location and is not raked. It need not be played at someone's home, nor be for small stakes. Indeed, one will stumble onto some very high stake home games.

Difference #1: The Rake

Casinos take a rake. This is done in a variety of ways. Ten percent of the pot to a maximum amount is common. A time charge is common – players pay a set amount each at a determined interval. Whatever the case, in a casino game you can be assured that the house is getting its piece of the action. As a matter of fact, there may be hidden costs. In casinos and card rooms where there is a bad beat jackpot, there is usually an extra rake. The house takes 10% to a maximum of $3 and they drop an extra $1 per hand that is added to the bad beat jackpot. The problem is, in some casinos there is a percentage charge on the bad beat as an administration fee. Thus, it's possible that the rake per hand is actually $3.30 ($3 plus 30% of the bad beat $1).

Home games do not have a rake. There is no house. You might be playing at Paul's house, but he is not *the* house. If Paul is taking a rake, you are probably in violation of your local law as just discussed. That is, if Paul is *pocketing* the rake. There is nothing illegal about a "pizza rake." One dollar from every pot goes to the pizza fund until there is enough cash to place an order. There is nothing illegal about that as nobody in particular is getting enriched. Just remember to wash your hands before you resume play.

Difference #2: The Rules

Rules are far from certain in home games. However, a couple of common themes prevail. Home games often do not permit check-raising. Many players consider check-raising to be rude. Home games often have different betting rules. Some home games, for instance, cap the betting at three raises, but do not require that a raise equal the previous bet. In a casino, all bets and raises must be at least as much as the previous bet. If a player bets $5, the next raise must be *at least* $5. It can be more, but it cannot be less. So in a three raise casino game, if player A bets $5, player B will have to fold, call the $5, or raise to $10. If the betting is capped then you will owe $20.

In home games where any size raise is allowed, player A bets $5 and player B then raises to $6. This can be a common tactic to slow the betting down in a situation where two players have very strong hands and want to keep on raising. One or more players who do not want a lot of money going into the pot simply put in the minimum bet as a raise. In a casino game the betting goes: A bets $5, you call, B raises to $10, A raises to $15, you call, and B caps it at $20. In a home game permitting undersize raises, the betting might go like this: A bets $5, you raise to $6, B raises to $11 and A raises to $16. By throwing in the $1 raise, you save yourself $4 compared to casino rules.

The long and short of it is that home games frequently have some odd rules. Casinos will differ from state to state, province to province, and country to country, but the rules will still be more the same than different. Home games can be very very different one from another even if they are on the same block. Make sure that you know the rules of the games before the cards are dealt.

Difference #3: The Skill Level

Even though the whole of this book talks about how poor the players generally are at low-limits in a casino, they are even poorer in home games. Casino poker players have usually played more hours than home poker players. No matter how poor casino poker players are, they consider themselves to be "serious" players. They still make countless mistakes, but they have learned by osmosis to avoid some of the worst errors. Consequently, casino poker is generally tougher than home poker.

Occasionally you might even stumble onto a home poker game that is so weak you have to slowly shear the sheep instead of killing them quickly. You will have to stop yourself from winning money so quickly that you are no longer welcome at the game.

Tim regularly played in a game at a local service club. The players were so weak that it was next to impossible for Tim to lose. Consequently he would take only $50 to a game in which most players were bringing $500. Of course, inevitably he got so unlucky that he lost his buy-in of $50. The other players where shocked to discover that $50 was all that he had been bringing to the game. After things folded up that night, the weak players got to chatting and they realized that Tim has been taking their money for a couple of years. He was no longer welcome in the game.

This is the phenomenon of there being "no sharks in the fish tank." If you take a group of poor players and have them play together, they will not realize they are poor players because no single one of them will be a consistent winner. One night player A will win, the next night B, and the next night C. Luck of the cards alone will determine the winner. In the long run, there are no losers and winners, they are simply trading around the same pool of money. If you introduce even a single skilled player into the mix, all of the equally bad players immediately become losing players. If you have one winning player, his win has to come from somewhere. It is coming from the other players in direct proportion to their skill level.

If you stumble upon a game in which the play is unbelievably weak, you may be well served to take the money at a slow and steady pace. If you win too much too quickly it will become apparent to the other players the "the new guy seems to win a lot" and you may find yourself out of the game.

Brent stumbled into just such a game. After a few sessions he managed to get an invite for Carson. Carson had a lucky evening and combined with the fact that he is a highly skilled player, he made $7000. Then he made a huge mistake. He left early. He quit before the game was done for the night. He was never invited back. The other players felt that it was rude of Carson to get ahead $7000 and then leave. You are wondering what is the problem with this story? Brent, who was slowly shearing the sheep, made $100,000 before the regulars in the game finally realized that there was a shark in the fish tank and stopped inviting him. For some home games, slow and steady wins the race.

Difference #4: The Size and Speed of the Game

In casinos, poker is usually played eight, nine, or ten handed depending upon the game and the location. Not so in home games. Most home games are smaller. The social element of the game is usually as important as the gambling portion. Consequently, the game goes ahead with less players. It is not uncommon to find home games with three, four, or five players maximum. There is also a simple restriction of space. Casinos have adequate space for a big ten handed hold 'em table. Most basements do not.

In a casino, the house supplies a dealer who has been trained and has dealt thousands of hands of poker. Moreover, the dealer will have dealt thousands of hands of hold 'em or whatever game you are playing at that moment. The house dealer is very likely to be quick. You can expect to play between thirty and forty hands of hold 'em per hour in a casino. Not so in a home game. In home games, the players deal. They are not trained and will come to the table with various degrees of skill. Some may not even be capable of a rifle shuffle. Consequently, the dealing is much slower. It is difficult to estimate how many hands per hour you will play in a home game. This will depend on a lot of factors. You can, however, be assured that home games will be slower than casino games.

Difference #5: Variety

There are very few poker variants offered in casinos. The big ones are hold 'em, omaha, omaha/8, 7-stud, and 7-stud/8. You will find these games at various limits, including of course pot-limit and no-limit. You will not, however, find much else.

Not so in home games. In home games the variety of games that are available are only limited by the imagination of the players. Most every variant will be based on the basic five card poker rankings, but this is where the similarity may end. Home games will feature High Chicago, Baseball, Indian Poker, and Spit in the Ocean. You will find Elevator, Fiery Cross, Guts, and In-between. You will encounter games with wild cards like dueces wild, one-eyed jacks wild, pregnant threes wild, and kings and little ones wild.

Variety and wild cards will contribute to the social atmosphere of the game. In part, this is because as you add more and more wild cards, you tend to increase the element of luck and decrease the element of skill. Everyone will be having a whale of a time tossing their money into the pot hoping for the best.

Difference #6: Availability

If you are in a jurisdiction that features casino poker, you will always have a game available. Simply slip down to the local casino and get in the game. The players will change from night to night, but there will always be a game. In fact, it requires changing players to sustain a game seven nights a week since nobody can play poker all the time (although you will meet those who try). My best guess is that a least thirty regulars are required to sustain a game for an extended period.

If you are in an area where there is no casino poker, finding a home game will be your only option. If you want to play more than one or two nights a week, you will be forced to find more than one home game. Remember, home games are as much social as they are about gambling. The participants are not likely to want to play more than once or twice per week. To that end, if you are in an area with limited access to casino poker then you have little hope of making your living playing poker or of truly developing your skills. To get better you have to play. A lot. Without a casino nearby, you will not have this opportunity.

Difference #7: Security

Casinos provide security. Not only in the literal sense of security cameras and security guards, but also in the form of lit parking lots and crowds of people. When you mix money and the human animal you sometimes get very unpleasant results. In the venue of a casino you are much less likely to be on the receiving end of an unpleasant situation. There are casino staff, patrons, and good lighting to get you safely to your car and safely home.

I have felt threatened three times in my brief poker history. Twice the situation was a home game in which I knew only one of the players and he was merely an acquaintance. In both cases I had made a small win, and in both cases I felt uncomfortable about leaving the game. The other event occurred right in the poker room at a major Las Vegas casino. I got into a war of words with another player and few moments later two burly young men positioned themselves directly behind me. In fact, they were leaning on the back of my chair. It appeared obvious to me that they were "employees" of the gentleman with whom I had had words. I left the game. They followed me out of the poker room and no further. So, despite the fact that I was intimidated into leaving the game I never felt overly threatened as I was in a casino with staff and security available to help me.

The point is that poker, like life, is not without risks. Doyle Brunson was once robbed on the doorstep of his home, presumably by thieves who followed him home from the casino. Take care of yourself. I doubt that you will have any trouble, particularly if you stick to low-limit poker. You should be aware of the fact that greed drives people to behave badly and you must protect yourself. If you have to pick, play in a casino where the atmosphere is controlled.

Difference #8: The Floor

Intimately related to the previous point, casinos have floor people while home games do not. In poker, there will inevitably be disputes. How should apparently conflicting rules be interpreted? Did Paul fold his hand or not? In a casino, when there is a conflict, the dealer will resolve it. If the dealer cannot, then the floor person will. There is an adjudicating body. Somebody will be left feeling annoyed (the floor has ruled against them), but as the sign on the wall says: "Decisions of the floor are final."

Not so in a home game. In a home game, when a conflict arises there is no house. The problem will probably be resolved by some vote or consensus of the players. There will still be somebody who is left feeling annoyed and he or she may never get over those feelings. He or she cannot direct his annoyance at a neutral third party like the floor person. He or she is forced to direct his annoyance at the other players. It makes for a very uncomfortable situation if the conflict is about a significant amount of money.

Difference #9: Friends and Enemies

Accept that there is going to be conflict in your poker game whether it is a home game or a casino game. There will be winners and there will be losers. Then, give some thought to the consequences. You will have more to lose in a home game because the conflicts, the wins, and the losses will arise between people who you are important to you – namely, your friends and family. In a casino, you may not even know the other players. The emotional consequences of hard feelings are considerably lessened in the casino environment.

Protect yourself from loss. In a home game, play with stakes that will not ruin relationships. Only you and the other players know how much this is. Do not exceed it. You cannot go home a winner – no matter how much money you make – if you destroy a relationship that has taken years to build. In the casino, on the other hand, beat them and trash talk them if you want to. It may be rude and obnoxious, but at least you are not hurting people that are important to you.

CHAPTER ELEVEN

TOURNAMENT POKER

Tournament poker is enjoying a huge and sustained explosion. Tournaments are popping up all over, at all limits. In 1995, Dan Harrington won The World Series of Poker Championship at Binion's Horseshoe in Las Vegas. To win, Dan bested a field of 273 players, each who paid $10,000 to enter. Dan won $1,000,000 for his efforts. In 2002 Robert Varkonyi was crowned the world champion of poker. Robert won $2,000,000. In a field of 631 players, the second place finisher (Julian Gardner) won $1,100,000. More than Dan won for winning the event a mere seven years earlier! The 2003 World Series of Poker Championship featured 839 players at $10,000 each. Chris Moneymaker won $2,500,000 for being crowned world champion. Impressive growth.

A quick review of the Card Player Magazine (www.cardplayer.com) website lists 94 weekly tournaments available in Nevada with buy-ins from $12 to $540. Another 120 weekly tournaments are available in California. Then there are at least fifty "major" tournament events that occur all over the world as multi-day events with hundreds of thousands, even millions of dollars in prize money. Not to mention online tournaments, and weekly tournaments outside of Nevada and California. Poker players love poker tournaments.

For the uninitiated, in a poker tournament you are eliminated when you lose all of your chips. To force the action, the betting limits increase at a timed interval. You cannot simply sit on your chips waiting and waiting for a huge hand because in short order, you will be eliminated by ever increasing antes and blinds. The tournament continues until one player has all the chips. The money is usually awarded according to a percentage payout schedule. For example, each player pays $100 to enter the tournament. If there are 100 players then the prize pool is $10,000. It is paid out 35% to first, 20% to second, 10% to third and 5% to each of 4th through 10th. First place would get $3500, second place $2000, and so on.

Most new poker players do not understand that playing a poker tournament is substantially different than playing in a ring game. Most beginning players simply start out playing their usual strategy and hope that luck will see them through. Poker tournaments are different and require you to adapt. This chapter will introduce you to some simple concepts that will get you started. This is, obviously, a very brief introduction to tournament poker. For a guide to literature specific to poker tournaments see *Chapter 15: Other Resources*.

Avoid Drawing Hands

Suited cards and connected cards are less valuable in a tournament than they are in a ring game. In a tournament, if you lose all your chips you are eliminated. Your chance of winning becomes zero. Not so in a ring game where if you miss a few of your draws you simply reach into your pocket and get out more money. In a tournament, you want to have the best hand *right now* or you want to be bluffing. You do not want to turn into a calling station. In tournaments, *bluff or have the best hand, but avoid drawing hands like the plague*. It is not unusual to miss three or four drawing hands in a row. In a ring game this is OK, but in a tournament you are eliminated. Good drawing hands are high variance. This means that although they are profitable in the long run, they will result in big swings over the short term. If one of those down swings breaks you, then you are out of the tournament.

As the Tournament Progresses, Players Get Tighter

In the early stages of a tournament, players have a lot of chips relative to the size of the antes or blinds. Consequently, the fear of going broke and being eliminated is not all that immediate. Most players will be playing their usual ring game style. As the tournament progresses, the size of the blinds and antes gets bigger and bigger to the point at which they feel oppressive. The fear of going broke becomes very immediate. Players get scared. When they get scared, they tighten up. They play fewer hands.

Bluffing Works Better in Tournaments

This is intimately related to the previous tip. Players get tighter. They play fewer hands *and* they get less inclined to call "just in case you are bluffing." So, as the tournament progresses bluffs are more and more likely to succeed. In low-limit poker it can be almost impossible to pull off a successful bluff. In big league tournament poker, you absolutely *need* to be able to make some timely bluffs.

Be Careful Near the End of a Limit or When Your Opponent is Desperate

The exception to the previous point is when you near the end of a betting limit. Suppose you are in a tournament with half-hour betting limit increases. You are five minutes from bumping up to the next level. The players are aware that their chips are about to get devalued (their stack will not go as far once the betting doubles). Thus, players are often looking for an opportunity to play a hand *now* as opposed to waiting five minutes for when the level increases. Similarly, many players get desperate when they get low on chips. They are looking for a chance to get their chips in and cross their fingers. The range of hands that they will play increases and they are more likely to call. They are harder to bluff.

Patience Patience Patience

The hackneyed expression in tournament poker is: "A chip and a chair." In other words, as long as you have not been eliminated, you still have a chance of winning. Players tend to panic too soon. Feeling the pressure of increasing blinds and antes, they give up too soon and shove their last chips into the fray with a marginal hand. Once you get low on chips, treat them like they are solid gold diamonds. Do not let them slip away.

Do Not Fall Behind the Curve

Having just told you to be very careful with your last chips, I will now tell you to gamble a little before you get desperately low. When you have almost no chips left, a lot of the weapons in your arsenal are taken away. For instance, the player with next to nothing will have a great deal of trouble pulling off a bluff. The time to gamble a little bit is not when you have next to nothing, but when you still have enough chips to be a threat. I try to always have at least the average number of chips in play at any given time. If I am in danger of falling behind the curve, I will look for an opportunity to take a reasonable gamble and get back in the fray.

Embrace Short-Handed Play

In tournaments you will play short-handed. Tables get short as players are eliminated. In fact, if you are to win the tournament, you will have to play heads up against the second place finisher! Most new players avoid short handed games as much as possible. If you are to succeed in tournament poker, you will have to learn to play against six, three, or even one opponent.

Make Deals

Often near the end of the tournament, the last three or four players will cut a deal. They will agree to divide the money in a way other than the "official results." I used to avoid deal making because I used to think I was a great player. I eventually learned two things: I am not that great a player and *no matter* how good I am, luck will matter *far more* than skill in the closing strokes of a poker tournament. Put your ego aside. Guarantee yourself as much money as you can negotiate. I see a lot of players overrate their skill in the late stages of a tournament.

Have Fun

Tournaments are a lot more pressure than ring games. As you get near the end, losing a hand does not feel like losing a few dollars. It *feels* like you are losing the whole first place prize money. Remember though, it is the pressure – the sweat and adrenaline – that *makes* it so much fun. Relax, drink it in and enjoy. Do not let the pressure get you down. It can. I know.

> *"Should I specialize in tournaments?" Paul asked.*
>
> *"Probably not," I answered. "If you want to make a living playing poker, depend on the side games to make your money. If you get a healthy bankroll and you have some extra cash, go ahead and take a shot at big tournament."*
>
> *"But the prize money is so huge, it seems a quick way to get rich."*
>
> *I nodded, "But the problem is, it is also the quickest way to go broke. Remember that you must have a bankroll big enough to support you and sustain you through your losing streaks. In tournament poker you can go on some very big losing streaks."*

Tip the Dealer

As much as you have felt the pressure, so have the staff. The tournament director, dealers, brushes, cocktail staff, etc have also felt the pressure. They have spent hours dealing with players in a pressure cooker. They have been doing their best. Give them a tip. I view it as our (the players) obligation to ensure that tournament poker will continue to grow and continue to attract excellent staff.

World Series of Poker

The World Series of Poker began in 1970. Benny Binion invited America's best players to the "World Series Of Poker" at his casino – Binion's Horseshoe Las Vegas – to crown the "World Champion." In 1970, there were only seven participants. The champion was determined by a vote. Johnny Moss became the first world champion.

In 1971 the winner was determined in a freezeout. The players put up their entry fees and the winner was the player who finished with all the chips. Johnny Moss did not need to get voted in. There were thirteen players total and Moss won it all.

In 1982, for the first time, the World Series of Poker exceeded fifty players (52). Just after that the World Series of Poker was expanded from a single event with a $10,000 entry fee to multiple events with varying entries. By 1987 the total entries in all events was over 2000. In 2002, there were over 7500 players. The total prize money in 2002 was $19,599,230, far exceeding the prize money for a PGA golf event. On May 23, 2003 Chris Moneymaker bested a field of 839 players and claimed the title of 2003 World Series of Poker Champion. Moneymaker entered a $40 online satellite tournament, won his entry fee, flew to Las Vegas, and left Binion's with his $2,500,0000 payday. Wow.

CHAPTER TWELVE

ONLINE POKER

Near the end of 1997, poker became available online. The first site of significance was planetpoker.com. By the end of 1998, online poker was common and the competition had begun. Today, online poker is a huge phenomenon. There are lots and lots of online sites, at least four of which are large sites with lots of games and limits to choose from. See *Chapter 15: Other Resources* for a rundown of the major sites.

How it Works

Generally the servers for online poker sites are "off shore." Online gambling is of dubious legality in most jurisdictions, so the servers are housed in countries which permit it. Because there is little that anyone in your jurisdiction can do to stop you from playing, the sites are thriving.

To play online, you start by making a deposit at the site of your choice. All the online sites do their transactions in U.S. dollars. There are a variety of ways to deposit money. Most commonly, you simply get out your credit card and make a deposit. The sites also offer online money management systems like Neteller, Firepay and Citadel Commerce. These are online "banks" that allow you to move money from your personal bank account into your online bank account, and ultimately into an online business. Neteller, Firepay, and Citadel Commerce are not used exclusively by online gamblers. You can make online consumer purchases with your online accounts as well. Online money management systems are the most convenient because they are the easiest way to move money between competing online poker sites. Online poker sites accept Western Union wire transfers. Finally, you can mail in your money. Once you have opened an account with the online poker site of your choice and made a deposit, you can begin playing.

Cashouts are done in reverse. If you made a credit card deposit, the site will refund your credit card up to the amount of your original purchase. If you made a deposit from one of the online "banks," your account will be credited the amount of your cashout. Finally, if you sent cash by wire transfer or mail, you will be sent a cheque.

I have had experience with several sites and I have never had difficulty with depositing funds or withdrawing them. I want to add here that I have no personal interest in any online site, nor have I been paid anything by any of them. This chapter is my candid opinion about online poker based upon my experience. I have played online practically everyday for the past six years. My advice is simple: stay with the big and well-established sites and you run next to no risk of being ripped off.

There is a practical side to the buy-in cash-out method of online poker. Since most players use their credit cards, it is impossible to fool yourself into believing that you are winning. Paul buys-in to an online site for $500 on his credit card. He plays the small limits for a couple of weeks and eventually goes broke. That $500 shows up on his credit card bill. Paul has never really gotten into the habit of keeping track of his wins and losses. This time, however, he is unable to deny his loss. There it is on his credit card.

In a live game, Paul walks into the casino with $500. He loses $200 and walks out. He spends the $300 in his pocket on clothes and takes more from the bank on his next trip to the casino. His poker money flows from his bank account, to his pocket, to the poker table, to his pocket, back to the poker table, to his pocket, to the pizza delivery guy. Without accurate records, Paul will never know if he is up or down because he will not know precisely where his money went. It is easy to convince yourself that you are a winning player when, in fact, you are not.

The result is that many players who *believe* they are winning in live game play find that they cannot win online. The truth is, they are losing players in live game play and they are simply continuing the trend online. The problem is, they think they are winning players. They have themselves so convinced that they are winners, that when they fail online, they complain that the online games must be fixed.

The lesson again is simple: keep track of all your wins and losses and then you will *know* if you are winning or losing.

How Online Games Differ from Live Games

In the first place, online poker is huge. As I type this, I am sitting at home on a Sunday evening. At this moment, there are over 10,000 players playing on the big three sites: partypoker.com, paradisepoker.com, and pokerstars.com. You can play limit hold 'em for as little as $0.50-1 or as much as $50-100. You can play pot-limit and no-limit hold 'em and omaha. You can play 7-stud from $0.50-1 to $10-20. You can play omaha-8, 7-stud/8, and one table tournaments. You can play multiple table tournaments. You can even play 5-stud, draw poker, and pineapple. In short, there are a lot of different games at a lot of different limits. Playing online offers you a *huge* selection of games and limits with almost no waiting.

Online games are fast. In the average live hold 'em game, you will play about 35 hands per hour. Lower-limit games are a little slower because there are more players seeing the flop, and the players play more slowly because they are not as experienced. Online, the average ten player hold 'em game plays about seventy hands per hour. Double the speed of live play. The reasons are obvious. Online play does not have any of the distractions or administration of live play. There is no shuffling, no cutting, no dealer changes, no player disputes, no cocktail staff, and no showboating. The game is crisp and quick.

The advantage to you is that if you play twice as many hands in the same time frame you should win twice as much money. If you average one big bet per thirty-five hands in live play, you should win two big bets per hour online. The disadvantage, of course, is that if you are a losing player then you will lose twice as fast.

Anything goes online. Well not anything, but you can get away with a lot that you could not get away with in live play. Do you want to have the starting hand guide from this book available to you while you play? No problem online. You could have your whole poker library at your finger tips and none of your opponents would know. Online you can (and should) take notes about your opponents while you play! In a live game you generally wait until after the game is done to take your notes. Online you can do it while you play. I once made notes for every single hand I played for a whole month. It was very educational. It is possible to do that in a live game, but it is much more convenient to do online.

Online games are tougher than live games. This is the most startling difference. If you are accustomed to playing in loose low-limit poker games, you are in for a surprise. There are a lot of things that contribute to making online games tougher. The biggest reason is that players who *think* they are winners in live games discover they are losers online. What do they do? They quit playing. Online play, much more so than live play, tends to have a Darwinian effect. The good players survive and the bad players disappear. Soon, instead of six fish there are only three, and then two, and then none. You are left with groups of skilled players requiring that you get beyond the basic skill set to beat the game. Mind you, this should not be exaggerated. Low-limits online are tougher than low-limits in live play, but they are still easy to beat using the basic strategy in this book.

I do not want to frighten you away from online play. I love it. I play online almost everyday. I have for six years. The online game can be beaten. All I am saying is that you should prepare yourself for the fact that the games are tougher than live play. For instance, at this moment on paradisepoker.com, I am looking at a 10 handed $1-2 limit hold 'em game in which only 22% of players see the flop. The average pot is being contested by two players, occasionally three. I defy anyone to find a micro-limit ten handed *live* hold 'em game in which only two players customarily see the flop. This does not happen in live games. Why is that? Better players. The bad ones have quit and the ones that are just learning are sitting at their computers with their books open and their thinking caps on.

Finally, online poker has very few tells. I find that in live play, I have a much better *feel* for my opponents. Despite taking copious notes about my opponents online, I still feel more in control in a live game. For me, it is mostly a matter of focus. I am better able to focus in a live game. At home, playing online, I am too tempted to check my email, read newsgroups, and bounce my son on my knee, all while playing poker. I have trouble staying focused online. You may not. I do.

The other reason that it is difficult to get a "feel" for the game online is that you are allowed to play more than one game at a time. Live, you are limited to one game. You are not allowed to run back and forth between two tables. You are not allowed to play poker while you also play blackjack. The expectation, rightfully so, is that you will give the game you are in your undivided attention. Not so online. Most every online poker site will let you play two or three games at once. The software is designed to automatically "pop" to whatever table needs your attention to the foreground of your computer screen. When it is your turn to act in the $3-6 hold 'em game, it pops to the foreground of your computer. Make your bet and continue to balance your cheque book. Next, your $1-2 7-stud game will pop to the foreground when you have to place your ante. In this way, you can play two or even three games at once. Login to two different sites and you could get four or even six games going at once. I don't recommend it, but it can be very tempting.

Are the Games Honest?

The honesty of online poker is a constant source of debate. There are two possibilities: the house is crooked and the players are crooked. Lets dispose of the first one. After several thousand hours of online play, I am confident that the house at all of the major sites is legitimate. There is no funny dealing going on. The game is not rigged. There are no "bots" playing in place of people. The house, online, is legit. I am confident of that.

Are the players cheating? There was a case early on in the history of online poker in which a major site was hacked. The security company that did the hacking was able to know, in advance, *every* players' cards. The security breach that caused the problem is fixed and there have been no reported instances of hacking since. This does not mean that it is not happening, it simply means that nobody is reporting it. This is a valid concern and one that you need to guard against. The best suggestion I have is (sounding like a broken record) "keep track of your wins and losses." You will *know* if you are winning or losing. If you are winning, then what is to worry about? If somebody is cheating and you are still winning then the cheat is not hurting you particularly. If you are winning then keep playing. If you are losing then quit. By quitting, you will protect yourself from the cheaters and you will protect yourself from the very real possibility that you are not a winning player.

I note here too that even if you are generally a winning player, you may go through periods of time in which you are off your game. During these down times, you may in fact be playing losing poker. This will be particularly evident online where there are more sharks waiting to eat you up when you falter. Time away will protect you from the remote possibility your opponents are cheating, but it will also protect you from continuing a losing skid brought on by poor play. Anytime you see a significant losing streak in your results, it is a good idea to step away and ask yourself, "Am I playing well and suffering a bad run of luck, or have I stopped playing well?" This can be a hard question to answer.

The biggest risk online is collusion. You can imagine one person who has two accounts. He could have both of his online "players" sit at the same virtual table. This would be cheating. Pure and simple. It could also go undetected. The cheater could do no more than use his two players as a means of knowing extra cards. So if one of his two players made a king high flush and his other player had the ace in the suit, he would *know* that his king high flush was the nuts. This little extra piece of knowledge alone would be sufficient to give the cheater an edge. If he really wanted to take advantage of the situation, he could use his two players to manipulate the betting in favor of his king high flush. He could raise and re-raise himself hoping to whipsaw the player in the middle for additional bets. Although more profitable in the short run, the cheater risks getting caught by doing this. If one is a committed conspiracy theorist, one can imagine a room filled with computer screens and player colluding like crazy.

Is there collusion happening online? Yes. Of course it is. Human nature being what it is, where there is an opportunity to get an edge, you will find people attempting to do just that. Colluding online is too easy, and human beings are too greedy. There is no doubt that collusion is happening online. Repeat, there is no doubt that collusion is happening online. However, collusion is also happening in live game play. There is no doubt that in poker, there is collusion. Constantly. Once there is money to be made you can count on the human animal to cheat. Greed is a powerful motivator. I feel certain that there is collusion online and live. The next question is, does it matter?

You can probably guess the answer: "Keep track of all your wins and losses." If you are religious about doing this you will know if you are winning or losing. If you see a long winning trend and then suddenly the trend turns down, it is time to stop and take notice. Analyze your play. If you feel strongly that you are playing winning poker and yet you are losing, quit. Take some time away from the game. Analyze your play. If you cannot find the leak, stay out of that game against those players. I am convinced that collusion is taking place both online and in live game play. I am also able to win both online and live. Is collusion hurting me? I do not know. If it is, it is not hurting me sufficiently to take me from winner to loser so I continue to play.

Interestingly enough, although collusion is easier to carry off online, it is also easier to catch. In live play, the house staff has no way of looking at players' cards surreptitiously to determine if there is any hanky-panky going on. Online poker rooms can quite easily check out all sorts things behind the scenes. Online, it would be fairly simple to automate a security system to catch colluders. As far as I know, none of the online rooms has done this. However, all of the big online cardrooms take allegations of collusion seriously and they will investigate all such complaints. There are numerous instances of players being banned and money being returned to players who were victims of collusion. In live play, if I accuse players X and Y of colluding, there is no easy way for the house staff to check my allegation. Online, the house staff simply looks behind the scenes at the cards that each player held and collusion may appear obvious.

The long and short of it is that online poker can be beat. I know many people who do. I know some people who have beat the online games for *a lot* of money. Just like live games, you must not overplay your bankroll, take precautions, and keep track of your wins and losses. Online poker is a great place to learn your trade since you can play for small limits like $1-2. If it is your only outlet, play the small limits. You will find that if you can beat an online $1-2 hold 'em game consistently, you will have no trouble beating a live $5-10 hold 'em game. Keep track. Study, practice, and repeat.

CHAPTER THIRTEEN

HOW TO KEEP IMPROVING

One: keep track of your results. If you are honest with yourself, you will be driven to improve. Two: study, practice, and repeat. If you genuinely want to become and remain a winning poker player, these two things alone, done unwaveringly, will get you there.

Study

You have already started to do this. You bought this book. If you are reading this chapter, you may have even read the bulk of this book. Having said this, reading is not adequate. You must *study*. You must engage your brain and constantly ask yourself, "What part of my game can I improve?" Reading a book once will not be enough. Read this book several times. *Think* about what you have read. Question it. Learn it. Consume it.

Studying means that you are actively working on getting better *away* from the table. You are doing things while you are not playing that will make you better. Chess masters do not only play chess, they study. Football players study video of the opposition to learn their strengths and weaknesses. Hockey players shoot thousands of pucks at empty nets. Army generals spend countless hours studying intelligence reports. If you want to get better at *anything*, you must be a lifetime learner. You must study.

"Study," in poker, means two things: read books and keep a journal. There are lots of good poker books available. Check the list in *Chapter 15: Other Resources* and start reading. A glance at the bookshelf beside me shows forty poker titles. I have a good collection, but it is not exhaustive. Go to your local library and start reading. Remember too that reading alone is not adequate. You must read critically.

I have taken certain liberties in this book. I have "rounded off corners" to create a simple, playable, and profitable formula for low-limit poker. As you gain a deeper understanding of the game, you will realize that every single hand you play presents different problems and opportunities. You will depart more and more from the "approximate" strategies described in this book (and others) and you will start to see poker as a fluid and creative game which cannot be given justice in an introductory tome such as this one.

Keep a journal. In addition to keeping track of your wins and losses, it is a simple matter to keep a journal. A narrative diary. Take notes. Contemplate them as you write them. Re-read them. Write down a hand or two from your last session and analyze the hand away from the combat zone. Did you play the hand well? Did you pay off a player when you should have known you were beat? Does Ernie have a tell? Make notes immediately after a session. Go back to them later and study them. Make it a point to learn something every time you play. Learn something about an opponent. Learn something about yourself. Learn something about the rules.

Find a mentor. Find someone that you trust and respect. Talk about hands of poker with that person. Go to one of the online discussion groups and pose your questions to a larger audience. Many writers and professionals are frequent contributors to various online discussions.

Practice

Practice online, practice with software, and practice when you play. You must not only be thinking about the game, you must be getting better at the table. All the theoretical knowledge in the world will not make you a winning player unless you are able to apply it. Focus on one or two elements of your game at a time. Do you know the starting hand guide by rote? Are you following it or is the gambling demon getting the better of you from time to time? Do you have a particular weakness for suited aces? Are your bluffs *always* getting called?

Perhaps you are bluffing too frequently or in bad situations. Decide that you will attempt only one bluff during your entire next session. Stick to your promise. Poker requires discipline. Perhaps you have a tell? Decide to work on making sure that you have a betting routine that minimizes the chance of giving off a tell to an astute opponent.

Practice the fundamentals. Repetition builds retention. The more that you do something, the more it becomes routine and the more likely you are to be able to successfully execute it under pressure. Ever try golfing? There is only one way to develop a golf swing. Repetition. Swing a golf club over and over again and eventually you will develop at least a passing ability to hit it. The key is that you *actively* practice. It would do you little good to hook yourself up to a machine that made you hit the golf ball unless you were being an active participant and concentrating. So it is with poker. Your *study* will help you decide what to practice, but your study will be of no value unless you actively make a point of practicing it.

Repeat

Even after you have been at it for some time, keep doing it. Even after your results show that you are a winning player, keep doing it. Even after you have made your million, keep doing it. If you want to get better at anything, you have to do the work. There is no substitute for preparation. *Fortes Fortuna Paratus Mens*. Fortune favors the prepared mind.

My Three Most Memorable Hands

I lost two of them and won one of them. They are memorable to me because they all occurred in high pressure situations with a lot of money on the line. I include them here for a couple of reasons. First, they are fun. Second, they are educational. I learned a lot in these three hands. I find myself, still, frequently contemplating the lessons learned.

Hand #1: The World Series of Poker 1998

I was attending the World Poker Industry conference that year. I was in Las Vegas for three nights and there was one World Series tournament available to me. $1500 7-stud-eight-or-better (7-stud/8) which is a variation of 7-stud in which the highest poker hand wins half the pot and the lowest poker hand wins the other half.

I had never played 7-stud/8 before in my life. Earlier that month I had won \$9,040 in a major Canadian tournament. I had the bankroll and I wanted to experience the World Series of Poker, so I decided to play in the tournament despite having never played 7-stud/8. For three weeks prior my departure, I studied 7-stud/8. I could not play 7-stud/8 live, it was not available online at the time, and there was no software available. Practice was hard, but I studied. Instead of "study-practice-repeat," I was left with "study-study-study". Luck smiled on me, and I made it past 242 players to get to the final table.

In the hand in question, I was the forced bring-in with (8♣-5♥)-2♥. Don Holt, the eventual second place finisher called with (X-X)-3♠. Tommy Hufnagel, the eventual winner, completed the bet with (X-X)-Q♣. I called. Holt called. By the time we got to 6th street, our hands looked like this:

Me:

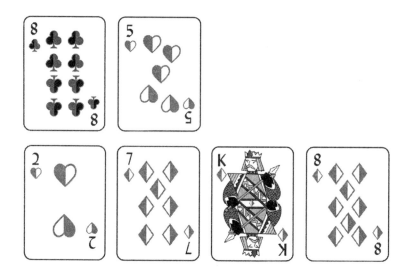

Don Holt:

Tommy Hufnagel:

Hufnagel checked. I checked. Holt bet. Hufnagel called. I raised. Holt re-raised. Hufnagel folded. I called.

I got exactly the result I was hoping for. I figured that Hufnagel would put me on a diamond flush or, at the very least, two pair better than his apparent pair of queens. On the river, I caught the 2♣ giving me a very weak two pair. Holt checked. I checked. He showed A♥-2♠-6♦ in the hole. Holt won the whole pot. That hand devastated my stack. I started the hand with $60,000 chips. I finished the hand with $30,000. I went on to finish in 5th place for a payday of $18,825, but I was *very* disappointed. First place paid $189,305. I did, however, learn two invaluable lessons.

In tournament poker it is very important to consider how *losing* a hand will effect you. I started the hand in 3rd chip position and finished the hand in 6th chip position. If I had been drawn out on I would not regret it, but I was not. I started with the worst hand, played it long past the point that I should have, made a last desperate bluff, and lost a lot of chips that I need not have lost. When you have a healthy stack of chips, it is often worth protecting. It is certainly not the time to be mixing it up with a marginal hand. That is exactly what I did. Remember the story of the General and the Dictator? I broke the cardinal rule. I entered the fray with an inferior force when there was no pressing reason to do so.

Perhaps more importantly, I learned that you should not step out of line unless you have a very good handle on the consequences. I was able to bluff Hufnagel out of the pot as I predicted, but I still had to *gamble* that Holt could not beat my meager pair of sevens. I felt certain that he had a low hand which I could not beat. In that case, the best I could hope for was to win half the pot. The other possibility is that I would lose the whole thing which is, of course, exactly what happened.

Hand #2: World Series of Poker 2001

In 2001 I played the $2000 no-limit hold 'em event. There were 441 player making 882,000 chips in play. With about forty players left I had 60,000 chips. The blinds were $1000-2000. It was folded to me two off the button and I made it $5000 to go with the J♣-9♥. The button called. Both blinds folded. I had a problem on my hands.

I did not know the button player. I had, however, played with him for about an hour and I knew he was capable of calling my pre-flop raise with almost anything. Several hands previous he called a raise from the player on my immediate left. He called another bet on the flop and then he bluffed all-in on the turn. He got lucky and rivered a gutshot to win the hand and bust the player on my left. It was obvious to me, however, that the button was a dangerous multi-dimensional player. He was a *Fox*.

The flop was K♥-T♣-9♦. I had bottom pair with a gutshot straight draw. I felt pretty certain that he did not have Q-J since it is a *very* poor hand in no-limit hold 'em. He would be much better off calling my raise with a big ace, pocket pair of any rank, or small suited connectors. I did not believe he had a pocket pair that had flopped a set because I felt he would have re-raised with any of K-K, T-T, or 9-9. I bet 15,000 hoping, of course, that he would fold. He did not. He called. The turn was the 4♣. The action was on me. I checked. He bet 20,000 and I folded.

The lesson I learned is that against certain types of opponents (Foxes) you have to decide to play the hand hard or not play at all. The button was capable of calling my flop bet of 15,000 with *nothing* just to see what I would do on the turn. I played right into the Fox's jaws. I bet once and then I checked and let him take me off a marginal hand. I did *exactly* what he wanted me to do. Three time world champion Stu Ungar is known to have said, "A lot of players can bluff once, but not a lot of players can bluff twice." I was only able to bluff once.

If I find myself in the same situation again – a Fox with lots of chips to act behind me – I will decide *on the flop* what to do. My feeling is that I should have checked the flop with the intention either of folding or check-raising all-in. Either option is superior to the weak way in which I played the hand.

The greatest lesson of the hand is the danger that skilled players with position on you present. To this day, I have no idea what I should have done on the flop or turn which is a tribute to the dangerous and tricky player who was the button. When you do not have a good handle on your opponent, he can manipulate you.

Incidentally, the top three finishers in the 2001 $2000 no-limit hold 'em event at the World Series of Poker were Phil Helmuth, TJ Cloutier, and Layne Flack. They are 2nd, 3rd and 27th on the World Series of Poker all-time money list with combined winnings of over 6.8 million dollars. At least I wasn't losing to some Screaming Fish! I finished in 27th place for a payday just over $5000.

Hand #3: Canadian Poker Championship 2002

We were down to the final six players at Casino Regina's 2002 Canadian Poker Championship. It was limit hold 'em, the blinds were $5000- $10,000, and I was the button. I started the hand with $120,000 chips. The average stack was $150,000. James Boxer, a dangerous player from western Canada raised under the gun. I held 7♠-5♠ and I re-raised him. The merits of this play are the subject of another book and are not the subject of this lesson. Both blinds folded. Boxer called. The flop was J♣-8♦-2♠. Boxer checked. I bet. I expected to pick up the pot at that point, but Boxer called. In know him to be a skilled player. I was certain that he was not calling with nothing. My feeling was that he had either flopped a set and was trapping me, or he had a pocket pair and wanted to see if I had the courage to bet again on the turn. I told myself "You are beat. You are finished with the hand. Your bluff has been unsuccessful. Do not lose any more chips."

The turn card was the K♥ and Boxer bet. This bet made me think. I felt certain that he did not have A-K since a few hands previously I had seen him go four bets pre-flop with precisely that hand. He did not re-raise me when I three bet him pre-flop so I doubted that he had A-K. I put him on a pocket pair. I figured that he was betting to find out how strong I was. I raised. Boxer folded Q-Q face up.

In the immediate aftermath of the tournament I was patting myself on the back for making a brilliant bluff. The lesson of the hand though is that luck matters more than anything in the short run. I got *unbelievably lucky*. There was only one way for me to win the pot and that was for a king to hit the turn. If any other card had come I would have folded to his bet or checked behind him and done the same on the river. It was a stroke of luck. Four outs in 46 cards. 10.5 to 1. I went on to finish first for a payday just over $26,000.

Conclusion

Study, practice, and repeat. Re-play hands over and over in your mind. Explore all the possibilities. Professional athletes call it visualization. Picture yourself swinging the bat and hitting a home run, and you will be more likely to succeed. In poker, picture yourself making calculated decisions in the heat or battle, and you are more likely to do just that. Picture yourself making judicious bluffs and you will do just that.

CHAPTER FOURTEEN

POKER PERSONALITIES

What follows is a short list of some of the prevalent people in the world of poker. This list is not exhaustive – it is skewed towards players that are active on the tournament circuit, particularly the World Series of Poker (WSOP). There are lots of excellent, professional players who rarely play tournaments. Tournaments are, by nature, very high variance. That is, you can go for long stretches without a significant win. You can of course, make a major score in a single day by winning a big tournament. Nevertheless, tournaments' high variance drives many pros to avoid them in favor of the more dependable income of side games. As a result, there are lots of excellent players who are not "known" since their names do not appear as tournament winners.

Doyle "Texas Dolly" Brunson

Seventy year old Doyle Bronson has played high stakes poker for most of his life. An all-star basketball player in high school, Brunson went to college and obtained a Masters Degree in Administrative Education. Intending to teach and coach, he quickly became enamored with the world of high stakes poker and has made his living from the game for his whole life.

One of only three players to have won nine WSOP events (Hellmuth and Chan are the other two), Brunson won the Championship in 1976 and 1977. Most recently, he added his 9th bracelet in 2003 winning the WSOP $2000 H.O.R.S.E. event (Prize: $84,080). His lifetime winnings at the WSOP are over $1.8 million.

Brunson is credited with ushering in the modern age of poker literature. In 1978 he wrote (with a group of collaborators) *Super/System* which is widely regarded as the first good "how to" poker book. It is still available and referred to often, particularly for its section on no-limit hold 'em which Brunson dubs "The Cadillac of poker games."

At the beginning of the 1998 movie *Rounders* Matt Damon's character is seen rummaging through his apartment pulling money out from every nook and corner to make up his poker bankroll. One of the sources is a copy of Brunson's *Super/System* into which he has tucked hundreds of dollars. Later in the movie Damon's character fantasizes about playing poker for a living at the Mirage in Las Vegas like Brunson. Still later in the movie, his character gets involved in a hand in which he has K-K and is thinking about what to do facing a big raise. He reasons that: "If my opponent has A-A I must fold, but if my opponent has anything else I should move all-in." In the movie, he moves in and wins the hand.

In a twist of "truth is stranger than fiction," Matt Damon played the 1998 WSOP Championship (basically to promote the release of Rounders). He wound up at the same table as Doyle Brunson and in a hand in which he had K-K he moved all-in only to get busted by Brunson who had A-A.

Johnny "The Orient Express" Chan

One of only three players to have won nine WSOP events (Brunson and Hellmuth are the other two). The forty-eight year old Chan has won the WSOP Championship twice, in 1987 and 1988. He tops the WSOP all-time money winners list with earning of almost $3.5 million. At the 2003 WSOP Chan won not one, but two events ($5,000 No-Limit Hold 'em and $5,000 Pot-Limit Omaha). Nolan Dalla has referred to Chan, correctly, as a "living poker legend."

Chan's family moved from Hong Kong to the United States in 1968. He began playing poker, as many do, in his teens for nickels and dimes. He attended the University of Houston (majoring in hotel and restaurant management), but did not complete his degree. In 1978 he moved to Las Vegas and took up gambling fulltime.

Chan made an appearance in the 1998 Matt Damon, Ed Norton poker movie Rounders. The movie used actual footage of Chan's confrontation with Eric Siedel from the 1987 WSOP as well as fictional footage of Chan in battle with Matt Damon's character.

Chan is, obviously, a very intimidating presence at the table not only because of his track record, but also his demeanor. In 1983, when Chan won $130,000 in Bob Stupak's America's Cup Tournament Stupak dubbed him "The Orient Express." He frequently has a "lucky orange" on the table in front of him. He has said that he likes the smell of the orange and it keeps him alert whilst trapped in the smoke of a casino.

There are now three active players with nine World Series of Poker bracelets: Chan, Hellmuth, and Brunson. Who will be the first to ten? Chan's personal website is www.chanpoker.com.

David Chiu

Winner of the Tournament of Champions in 1999 at which he made a much celebrated pre-flop fold of K-K (his opponent showed A-A after Chiu folded). He has won three WSOP bracelets.

T. J. Cloutier

Sixty-four year old Texan T. J. Cloutier is one of the most successful long-term players on the tournament circuit. Cloutier has won four WSOP events and come very close to winning the Championship five times (two seconds, one third, and one fifth). He was won over $3 million at the WSOP.

Weened as a Texas road gambler, Cloutier's books feature pages of colorful apocryphal tales of playing poker for a living on the road. Of particular interest to Canadian poker fans, Cloutier was a linebacker with the Montreal Alouettes of the Canadian Football League in the early 1970's.

Cloutier's self-proclaimed photographic memory is legendary. In fact, Daniel Negreanu (another world class tournament pro) has this to say about Cloutier: "I believe this to be one of T. J. Cloutier's biggest strengths. He has enough faith in his instincts that he is capable of making plays that appear to defy logic. It's tough to argue with the most successful tournament player in poker history."

Cloutier has co-authored (with Tom McEvoy) three books: Championship No Limit and Pot Limit Hold 'em, Championship Omaha Pot Limit, Limit, 8 or Better, and Championship Hold 'em - Limit.

Allen Cunningham

At 27, Cuningham is one the crop of superior younger players. To quote Nolan Dalla: "Young and brilliant... Despite his young age, he knows as much about no-limit hold 'em as any man alive." Winner of the 2001 WSOP $5000 7-stud event.

Nolan Dalla

Forty-one year old Nolan Dalla is both a professional gambler – poker and sports handicapping – as well as a writer. Dalla graduated from the University of Texas in 1984 and pursued a career with the US State Department. While working at the American Embassy in Bucharest, Romania he witnessed the fall of dictator Nicolae Ceausescu and the end of Communism in Eastern Europe. He was the first American to establish contact with the revolutionary government inside the Communist Party's Central Committee Building on December 22, 1989. He also hosted one of Eastern Europe's most popular poker games on the diplomatic circuit.

Dalla was a columnist for CardPlayer for eight years and created the "Player of the Year" ranking system used by the magazine since 1997. For the last several years Dalla has handicapped the WSOP Championship. His WSOP odds and writings can be found every April at www.pokerpages.com.

Dalla hosts a free sports handicapping service at www.madjacksports.com. He is also the lead sports gambling writer for both Casino Player and Western Player Magazine. He also does consulting work for casinos and is currently involved in a major project for Binion's Horseshoe in Las Vegas.

Layne "Heart Attack" Flack

Thirty year old Layne Flack has won five WSOP events including two events at the 2003 WSOP – $2500 Omaha-8 (Prize: $119,260) and $1500 Hold 'em Shootout (Prize: $120,000).

Born in South Dakota, Flack grew up in Montana. At the age of nineteen he was the night manager at a Billings casino. Inspired by his early success in management he went to college to study business management but soon found that he was making too much money playing cards to stay focused on his education. His skyrocketing career as a poker pro took off instead.

Noel "J.J." Furlong

Another player from the "super aggressive" school of thought. 64 year Irishman, Furlong is a businessman first, and poker pro second. Furlong won the 2001 WSOP Championship. In the most memorable hand from the final table Huck Seed (1996 WSOP Champ) called $20,000, Furlong raised it to $100,000, the blinds folded, and Seed moved all-in. Furlong called. Seed held J-8 and Furlong held A-3. Furlong's comment later was "I had my thumb on Seed the whole previous day."

Jennifer Harman

Harman won the 2000 WSOP $5000 no-limit deuce-to-seven event. More impressive, she had never played the game before that day. Obviously, a superior player. One of the best in the world and certainly one of the top women in the world.

"Action" Dan Harrington

In 1995 Harrington won the European championship, a preliminary WSOP no-limit event, and the WSOP Championship. He followed that remarkable year by winning the $5,000 no-limit tourney at the Four Queens in 1996. Harrington is a 57 year old former bankruptcy lawyer. As a young man he was a state chess champion and backgammon professional. He moved to Las Vegas full time in 1990.

Phil Hellmuth, Jr.

Thirty-nine year old Hellmuth is one of only three players to have won nine WSOP events (Brunson and Chan are the other two), including the Championship in 1989. Most recently Hellmuth won his eighth and ninth bracelets at the 2003 World Series winning the $2500 limit hold 'em event (Prize: $171,400) and the $3000 no-limit hold 'em event (Prize: $410,860). He also came close in the 2003 WSOP Championship finishing 27th out of 839 (Prize: $45,000). With a substantial chip stack he went out in consecutive hands when his Q-Q lost to J-J and his A-K lost to A-J. Both bad beats.

There is no doubt that Hellmuth is one of the best tournament players in the world. Quite possibly the best. His skill at reading his opponents is beyond compare. Hellmuth does have something of a legendary temper, but he appears to have reigned it in recently and is generally an elegant and gracious ambassador of the game.

In 2003 Hellmuth wrote *Play Poker Like the Pros* which is an introduction to many popular poker variants as well an introduction to tournament strategy, online strategy, etc. His personal website is www.philhellmuth.com.

Phil Ivey

Young and very talented. Ivey has set his sights on being "the best player in the world" and his early results indicate that he is well on his way. He is among the most aggressive players in the tournament circuit.

Linda Johnson

49 year old ex-publisher of CardPlayer Magazine. Johnson continues to operate CardPlayer Cruises and hosts the annual World Poker Conference (annually in Las Vegas). She started playing poker in 1974. Johnson is often sited for her superior promotion of poker. A class act in every way. Winner of the 1997 WSOP Razz event.

Berry Johnston

Has finished in the money over forty times at the WSOP. He won the Championship in 1986. An elegant, soft spoken gentleman at the table.

Lou Krieger

Lou Krieger is one of poker's most prolific and elegant writers. He is a regular player in Southern California's $15-30 and $20-40 games. He is a regular columnist with CardPlayer Magazine, Western Player Magazine, Casino Player, and pokerpages.com. He is also the host of royalvegaspoker.com

Krieger was born in Brooklyn, but now resides in Palm Springs, California. He learned poker as child in his family kitchen and his New York roots remain. He is the captain of the Coney Island Whitefish BARGE team. Ask him what a Coney Island Whitefish is the next time you are in a game with him.

Krieger's books include Hold 'em Excellence, More Hold 'em Excellence, Poker For Dummies, Gambling For Dummies, and his most recent Internet Poker: How to Play and Beat Online Poker Games.

Howard Lederer

One of poker's best high-stakes players. Early in 2002 he decided to dedicate himself to no-limit hold 'em tournaments. Good choice. Lederer won two World Poker Tour events. First played the WSOP Championship is 1987 which remains his best finish (5th). In 2003 he finished in 19th place in the big one although he did win a bracelet in 2001. Has has been called "The Professor" probably due to him demeanor at the table.

Carlos Mortensen

2001 WSOP Champion. Has a reputation of being very aggressive. At the 2001 final table Mike Matusow raised it to $60,000 before the flop and Mortenson re-raised to $150,000. Matusow then re-re-raised to $350,000 and Mortensen moved all-in. Matusow folded and Mortensen showed Q-8o! Do you think bluffing and reading your opponent plays an important role at the WSOP level? Mortenson, from Madrid, Spain, has been a pro since 1997.

Daniel Negreanu

A twenty nine year old Canadian who now lives in Las Vegas, Nevada. Negreanu burst onto the scene in 1997 when he won "Best Overall Player" at the World Poker Finals, Foxwoods Resort and Casino and quickly followed that in 1998 by winning the WSOP $2000 pot-limit hold 'em event (Prize money: $169,460). At age 23, he was the youngest ever WSOP winner. Most recently, Negreanu won the 2003 WSOP $2000 S.H.O.E. event.

Like a rock band or a pop singer, "burst on the scene" actually means "had his years of hard work finally rewarded with wide public acclaim." As with most "overnight sensations" there are usually years of hard work before they are "discovered." Negreanu played professionally in Toronto and area for years before he was "discovered".

Widely considered to be one of the best tournament players in the world, Negreanu writes a regular column for CardPlayer Magazine and is a frequent contributor to the poker newsgroup rec.gambling.poker. At tournament time he is usually attired in the jersey of an NHL hockey team. His personal website is www.fullcontactpoker.com.

Men "The Master" Nguyen

Forty-nine year of Nguyen (pronounced "win") started playing poker in 1985. He has been at over twenty final tables at the WSOP and won four WSOP events (never the "big one" though). He won the 2001 Tournament of Champions poker match at the Trump Taj Mahal in Atlantic City (Prize: $280,000).

Nguyen quit school at age thirteen. He arrived in the United States in 1978 having escaped the communists in Vietnam. He worked a variety of menial jobs until discovering poker at Caeser's Palace in 1985.

Nguyen is, perhaps, the most controversial regular player on the major tournament circuit. Nguyen teaches and finances a group of Vietnamese players, in exchange for which he takes a percentage of their wins (probably 50%). Whereas there is nothing wrong with this in principle, it comes with frequent rumors of collusion surrounding Nguyen and "his boys." There is a saying in jurisprudence that "justice must not only be done, it must be seen to be done." If there are three of you left in a tournament – you, Nguyen, and one of "his boys" – will you be getting a fair shake? You may, but it will not feel as though you are. It will feel as though you are playing against a team that is colluding to beat you. None of these rumors have ever been proven, but they persist.

"The Master" nickname comes from one of his students who gave him the name in 1991.

Scotty Nguyen

The 1998 WSOP Champion. He has three WSOP victories in total.

David "The Dragon" Pham

CardPlayer Magazine's 2000 "Player of the Year." Pham won the 2001 WSOP $2000 S.H.O.E. event. He is the best known student of Men "The Master" Nguyen. A businessman, he turned poker professional in 1998.

Huck Seed

The 1996 WSOP Champion, he was 27 when he won it making him the youngest player to ever with the championship event. Seed was studying electrical engineering at Cal Tech, but took a leave of absence in 1989 to play poker and never returned to school.

Erik Seidel

One of the most successful players in WSOP history with six bracelets, most recently he won the 2003 WSOP $1500 pot-limit omaha. He has made the final table in the WSOP Championship twice – fourth in 1999 and second in 1987 (the footage in the 1998 movie Rounders is actual footage of Chan beating Seidel in 1987).

Barry Shulman

Fifty-seven year old Shulman is the publisher of CardPlayer Magazine. Shulman is not only a poker publisher but is also a very competent player. He has one WSOP bracelet.

Dewey Tomko

A onetime kindergarten teacher, Tomko is a world class senior golfer (he used to manage the Southern Dunes Golf and Country Club in Haines City, Florida which he co-owned with Benny Binion and Doyle Brunson). He finished second in the WSOP Championship in 2001 and 1982. An enduring high-stakes player who limits himself to big tournaments.

Dave "Devilfish" Ulliott

Probably the best known player from the UK. Winner of the 1997 WSOP $2000 pot-limit hold 'em (Prize: $180,310) and most recently, in January 2003, he won the Main Event at the 4th Annual Jack Binion World Poker Open (Prize: $589,990). Ulliott boasts many other tournament victories and WSOP close calls.

A jeweler by trade, Ulliott can be recognized by his rings. On his right hand over his middle and ring fingers he wears a gold ring reading "Devil" and on his left hand a similar ring reads "Fish." His nickname was given to him by opponents in Birmingham, England as a reference to the Chinese culinary delicacy which, if not properly prepared, can kill you.

Ulliott is a regular player on the major tournament circuit. He is known as a very aggressive player and frequently puts his opponents to some very difficult decisions.

Stu "The Kid" Ungar

Generally regarded as the greatest no-limit hold 'em player of all time. He won the WSOP Championship three times: 1980, 1981, and 1997. He also won the $10,000 event at Amarillo Slim's Superbowl of Poker three times. After a too-short life plagued with drug addiction, Ungar died in 1998 at the age of forty-two. Nolan Dalla has written a complete biography of Stu Ungar, *The Man Behind the Shades: The Life and Times of Stuey the Kid Ungar.*

His nickname comes from the young age at which he entered the world of high stakes poker. Ungar was just 24 when he won the WSOP Championship in 1980. Young hot shot players have become common now, but in 1980 high stakes poker was heavily dominated by the "old school."

Amazingly, Ungar only turned to poker after Gin Rummy dried up. In the late 1970's he played Gin Rummy in New York and Las Vegas for any amount of money against anybody. Soon, he could not get a game because nobody was willing to play him. He was forced to take up poker just to stay in the action.

CHAPTER FIFTEEN

OTHER RESOURCES*

Books

Big Deal: One Year as a Professional Poker Player, Anthony Holden.
Not a "how to" book. A brilliant, funny and poignant non-fiction account of one year on the tournament circuit. Holden is a brilliant writer.

The Biggest Game in Town, A. Alvarez.
Not a "how to" book. A fascinating look at the world of high-stakes poker in Las Vegas and in particular the World Series of Poker.

Caro's Book of Tells, Mike Caro.
The definitive work on tells. Practically the only book on tells. Thorough and essential to your continued education.

Caro's Fundamental Secrets of Winning Poker, Mike Caro.
A mixed nuts book that covers all sorts of things. Caro is a great writer. His books are fun to read and generally filled with all sorts of useful information. He is also a great speaker. If you get the chance to attend a Mike Caro poker seminar, do so.

Gambling Theory and Other Topics, Mason Malmuth.
Not a "how to" book, but it is filled with indispensable information on many topics with which you should be familiar if you are to be successful as a gambler, including a thorough discussion on bankroll requirements.

*Nobody listed here has paid anything to the author, nor does the author have any interest herein.

Hold 'em Excellence, Lou Krieger.
The best writer among poker scribes. This book and its companion More Hold 'em Excellence are an elegant and thorough introduction to winning at hold 'em.

Hold 'em Poker For Advanced Players, David Sklansky and Mason Malmuth.
As the quote on the back cover says: "The definitive work on hold 'em poker." This book is thorough and correct. You must become familiar with the contents of this book. Your skilled opponents will be.

Improve Your Poker, Bob Ciaffone.
A very excellent, practical manual that introduces a lot of poker concepts in a neat and tidy package.

Poker Nation, Andy Bellin.
"A raucous journey into the shut-up-and-deal world of professional poker." An informative look at the thrills and pitfalls of playing for a living.

Poker Tournament Tactics for Winners, D.R. Sherer.
An excellent approach to tournament poker. If you get only one tournament poker book, get this one.

The Secret to Winning Big in Tournament Poker, Ken Buntjer.
A step by step methodology for approaching poker tournaments. It is also the only other place that I have seen a thorough player classification system.

7 Card Stud, Roy West.
The best beginner book for 7-stud. The sub-title is How to win at Medium and Lower Limits. If you are a beginning 7-stud player, this is the book to get.

Seven Card Stud For Advanced Players, David Sklansky, Mason Malmuth and Ray Zee.
Also thorough and correct. The best book for those wanting to get to advanced levels of play in 7-stud.

The Theory of Poker, David Sklansky.
This book is indispensable. If you want to grow into a skilled, dangerous player in any form of poker you will need to study this book. It gives you

all of the principles upon which your successful poker career will depend.

Tournament Poker For Advanced Players, David Sklansky.
Another brilliant and thorough book from Sklansky. If you intend to compete in any "major" tournaments this book is an excellent manual.

Winning Low-Limit Hold 'em, Lee Jones.
A brilliant book for hold 'em novices. A thorough study of this book will make you a winning player at low-limit hold 'em.

Software

Pokerwiz.
The complete poker simulation wizard. Runs Monte Carlo simulations allowing you to specify the game, players, hands, etc. A very useful tool. Available at www.pokerwiz.com.

StatKing, ConJelCo.
Poker results tracking tool. You are able to sort your results by game, location, and date. Computes your win-rate, confidence, and standard deviation. Includes graphing, advice, bankroll requirements, streak analysis, and much more.

Tournament Texas Holdem for Windows, Wilson Software.
Enables you to set the tournament size, limits, blind structures, number of rebuys, etc. An excellent program with which to practice your tournament play.

Turbo 7-Card Stud for Windows, Wilson Software.
Play against 2 to 7 players, interactively or with high speed simulations. Set limits, bring in method, bet amounts, etc. Extensive statistics. Play evaluation, optional bring-in, peek, enhanced graphics, sound, printing, and statistics. The state of the art software to practice and research.

Turbo Texas Hold 'em for Windows, Wilson Software.
The most powerful and easy to use hold 'em program available. Create players with individual playing styles. Set limits, blinds rake, tokes, etc. Extensive statistical reporting, high speed simulation. Enhanced graphics, sound, animation, enhanced data charts, printable player profiles.

Online Poker Sites

Online sites frequently offer sign on bonuses (free money) and special promotions. Once you download a site's software, you will be on the mailing list and you will be notified of any special promotions they have. All of them offer "play-money" games so that you can practice at no monetary risk.

paradisepoker.com
The first huge online poker site. It has recently fallen to third place, but still boasts thousands of players at a huge variety of games and limits.

partypoker.com
Lots of games. Lots of limits. Offer the "Partypoker Million" which is an online tournament culminating in a live tournament on a Card Player Cruise with prize money in excess of $1 million. Hosted by Mike Sexton "World Famous Poker Pro." The biggest online poker site.

pokerstars.com
Lots of games. The online leader for multi-table tournaments. Hosts the World Championship of Online Poker every August.

planetpoker.com
The first poker site. It still boasts a small, committed core of players. Hosted by Mike Caro "The Mad Genuis of Poker."

ultimatebet.com
Home of the biggest money games online.

Other Online Resources

binions.com
The home of the World Series of Poker.

canadianpoker.com
The author's homepage.

canadianpokerplayer.com
Canada's national poker magazine.

conjelco.com
The best online supplier of gambling books, videos and software. If you intend to order anything gambling related, this is a terrific site.

pokerpages.com
An excellent online stating point. A melting pot of tips, articles, schedules and more.

pokerschoolonline.com
An excellent online school. Lou Krieger, Nolan Dalla, Daniel Negreanu, and Mike Caro are just some of the instructors.

twoplustwo.com
The home of Two Plus Two Publishing, publishers of David Sklansky and Mason Malmuth. The site features and excellent online message board with beginner and advanced "conversations" about all aspects of poker.

wilsonsoftware.com
The best poker software available.

wsop.dk
The ultimate site for links. Start here and you will find your way into almost every online poker site out there.

GLOSSARY

Action: Betting. If someone says "there has been action," they are saying that there has been a bet. Also, the player who's turn it is to act is said to "have" the action. For example, "The action is on you Paul."

Add-on: At the end of the re-buy period in a poker tournament, there may be one final opportunity to add-on. That is, one final opportunity to purchase a set amount of tournament chips for a set amount of money.

All-in: When a player puts the last of his money in the pot he is all-in. The all-in player is not eligible to win money in excess of what they have placed in the pot themselves. So, if Albert, Bob, and Paul start the hand with $50, $50, and $10 respectively, the most that Paul could finish with is $30 (his own $10 plus $10 from each of Albert and Bob).

Ante: A forced bet. Each player posts an ante. The combined antes make up the pot prior to the first betting round.

Betting Round: The series of bets or checks made in turn by all eligible players before more cards are dealt or there is a showdown. For example, in hold 'em there is a "betting round" between the flop and the turn.

Bicycle: The same as a bike. A straight to the five (A-2-3-4-5).

Big-bet: In a fixed-limit poker game, the larger of the two bets. In $10-20 hold 'em the big bet is $20.

Bike: A straight to the five (A-2-3-4-5).

Blind: A forced bet. In hold 'em there is usually a small-blind to the immediate left of the button and a big-blind immediately to the left of the small-blind. They generally replace an ante and define the betting for the first betting round. Also, a blind bet. You will frequently hear players say "I check blind," meaning that they are checking before they see the next card or cards (be it the flop, turn, 6th street, or whatever).

Bluff: A bet with a hand that you do not believe is the best hand. When you bluff you are hoping that all of your opponents will fold and you will be awarded the pot since you are the sole remaining player.

Board: Either the community cards in hold 'em or the up cards of a player in 7-stud. If a player "plays the board" in hold 'em, his poker hand consists of the five community cards and neither of his hole cards.

Boat: A full house.

Broadway: A straight to the ace (T-J-Q-K-A).

Brush: The house staff person who is taking care of the seating list. He will ensure that games are filled in an orderly fashion. In small cardrooms the brush, chip runner, and floorperson positions are often filled by a single person.

Button: An object on the table (usually a plastic disk) marking which player is the virtual "dealer." Also used to denote that player. "Paul is the button." The button acts last and is the most desirable seat since you will have position on your opponents throughout the hand.

Buy-in: The minimum amount of money that one must put up as their table stake to be allowed to play. Frequently, it is ten times the small bet. In a $10-20 hold 'em game the buy-in will be $100. In a poker tournament, it is the amount of money that you must put up to play. The World Series of Poker Championship boasts a buy-in of $10,000.

Call: To equal the amount of the previous bet.

Cap: To put in the final raise. In a game with a maximum of three raises, the player who puts in the third raise "caps it."

Cards speak: The best hand will be awarded the pot. You do not need to declare your hand, your cards speak. The dealer will figure out who has the best hand.

Check: To pass the action to the next player without putting any money in the pot. This option is only available where you are the first to act, or where there has not yet been a bet.

Chip runner: The house staff person who gets chips for a seated player.

Dealer: The house staff person who is dealing the cards and running the game. In hold 'em the player with the button might also be called the dealer.

Doorcard: In 7-stud, a player's first faceup card is his doorcard.

Draw: The hand you are hoping to

develop. If you have a "flush draw," you do not yet have a flush, but there are more cards to come and you might still get your flush. You are "drawing" for a flush.

Fifth street: In 7-stud, it is the fifth card (the third faceup card).

Fixed-limit: A betting structure in which all bets and raises are at the fixed amount. So, in $5-$10 hold 'em the first two betting rounds feature bets and raises of $5 and last two betting rounds feature bets and raises of $10. You cannot bet $4 or $9. Betting is "fixed."

Flop: In hold 'em, there are five community cards. The first three cards are turned faceup at the same time. These three cards are the flop.

Flush: A poker hand consisting of five cards from the same suit.

Fold: To discard your hand. If you fold you have no chance of being awarded the pot.

Forced bet: A bet which must be made. In hold 'em, the big-blind and small-blind are forced bets. In 7-stud, the player with the smallest door card must make a forced bring-in bet to start the action.

Full house: A poker hand consisting of a three-of-a-kind and a pair.

Gutshot: A straight draw in which there is one specific card required to make the straight. For example, 9-8-6-5 and A-K-Q-J are both gutshots. There is one card needed for a straight, namely a seven in the first case and a ten in the second case.

Hand: Both the particular cards held by a player (his "hand") and the play of one "game" of poker, including everything from the dealing of the cards to the awarding of the pot.

Heads-up: A hand with only two players remaining. In many cardrooms, once a pot becomes heads-up there is no limit on raises.

Heater: A series of hands in which one player is winning more than his share. "Paul sure got on a heater last night." You will also hear that a player is "hot," meaning that he is on a heater.

Hold 'em: The usual, although shortened name for "Texas hold 'em." A form of poker in which each player makes a five card poker hand by combining his two pocket cards with five community cards in the center of the table.

Hole cards: Your first two cards in 7-stud. Your two cards in hold 'em.

House: The casino or cardroom. It refers to the location and staff. The brush, chip runner, dealer, and floorperson are the house staff.

Inside straight: Same as a gutshot.

Jackpot: Many cardrooms offer a bad beat jackpot. When a particular set of criterion are met then the jackpot is paid. A hold 'em jackpot might have the following criterion: aces full of jacks must lose and both players must use both their hole cards.

Kicker: The card in your hand that will be used to break a tie. Common in hold 'em. If one player holds A-K and the other player A-J, the first player will win because his king is a "bigger kicker."

Kill: In a "kill" game, when one player wins two pots in a row, the betting limit for the next hand will be increased. "The kill is on." In a $10-20 hold 'em game, if there is a "half-kill" then when one player wins two pots in a row the game will be $15-30 for the next hand. If there is a "full-kill," the game will be $20-40 for the next hand.

Limit-poker: A betting structure in which there is a strict limit on the amount you can bet. Limit poker can be played fixed or spread limit.

Limp: To enter a pot for the minimum. Calling the forced bet is "limping in."

Loose: A game can be loose or a player can be loose. In either case there are too many hands being played. A loose player plays too many hands. A loose game means that several players are playing loose.

Main pot: At the beginning of a hand all players are eligible to win the main pot. If a player runs out of money and goes all-in, he will remain eligible for the main pot and the other players will be contesting the main pot and the side pot.

Monte Carlo: A gambling Mecca, but also a type of simulation in which all future possibilities are tested.

Muck: The pile of cards made up of the discards. If you fold, you "muck" which is to say you put your cards with the discards.

No-limit: A betting structure in which the only limit on the amount a player can bet is the amount of money he has as his table stake. No-limit and pot-limit are sometimes referred to as "big bet poker."

Open: It is the first bet. If you make the first bet, you "open" the betting.

Open-end straight draw: A straight draw in which either one of two cards will complete the straight. For example, 8-7-6-5 is an open-end straight draw since either a nine or a four will make a straight. Also called an "open straight draw."

Option: In hold 'em, the big blind can raise even if no other player has. He has the "option" of raising. This is the only time when a player may bet (albeit a forced bet), get called, and then still put in a raise.

Over button: In some games, players can take an over button. If only players with over buttons remain in the pot, the game switches to an agreed higher betting limit. Suppose you are in a $10-20 hold 'em game. Six players have over buttons and four do not. If all four of the players without over buttons drop out, the six remaining players will switch to $20-40 for the remainder of that hand.

Pair: Two cards of the same rank. When combined with three other non-matching cards it is the five card poker hand "one pair."

Pocket: Your face down cards. In hold 'em and 7-stud, they are the first two cards dealt to you.

Position: Your place in the order of betting. You are said to "have position" on an opponent if you act after him. Players behind you "have position" on you.

Post: To place your small-blind or

big-blind bet in hold 'em. Usually in hold 'em if you are a new player in the game you will be made to post a big-blind. You can wait until it is your natural turn to post the big-blind or you may post it early and get in the game for the current hand.

Pot: The money that has been contributed, through betting, by all the players. The pot is awarded to the player who remains "in the pot" and has the best hand at the showdown. If only one player remains, there is no showdown and the sole remaining player is awarded the pot.

Pot-limit: A betting structure in which a bet or raise may be up to the amount of the pot. For example, if the pot is $2 then Paul can bet $2. Larry can then raise to $8 (he calls the $2 and raises the amount of the pot which is now $6). Paul could re-raise to $28 ($8 plus the $20 in the pot) and Larry could re-re-raise to $96 ($28 plus the $68 in the pot). No-limit and pot-limit are sometimes referred to as "big-bet poker."

Pot odds: That ratio of the amount of money in the pot to the size of the bet. If there is $100 in the pot and you must call $10, your pot odds are 10 to 1.

Raise: To raise the bet from its

current level. Raising is not an option until the betting has been opened. In a $6-12 7-stud game with a three-raise maximum, you could pay $24 in a $6 betting round. Opening bet $6, one raise to $12, two raises to $18, and three raises to $24.

Rake: The money that the house takes from the game. At low-limits, the rake is usually taken every hand and typically as a percentage to a maximum. For example, the house might take 10 percent to a maximum of $3. If the pot gets to $30, the house will get $3, but any money that goes into the pot after that will not be raked.

Re-buy: When poker tournaments allow players to buy more chips after the start, these chip purchases are called re-buys. They will only be allowed for a set amount of time. A poker tournament without re-buys is called a freeze out.

Re-raise: Any raise after the first raise. Paul bets $10, Larry raises to $20, and Steven "re-raises" to $30.

River: The final card. In hold 'em, it is the fifth card on the board. In 7-stud, it is the 7th card received by a player.

Royal flush: A poker hand consisting of A-K-Q-J-T of the same suit.

Runner-runner: A hand that is made by drawing two required cards one after another. In hold 'em, if Paul has A-K and the flop is T-7-2, then he will get a "runner-runner straight" if the turn is a Q and the river is a J.

Rush: Same as a heater. When a player wins more than his share over a few hands, a few hours, or an evening, he is said to be on a "rush."

Scare card: A card which looks likely to have improved your opponent's hand.

Set: Three-of-a-kind.

Showdown: Starting with the last player to open or raise, players turn their hands face up. The dealer awards the pot to the winner of the showdown which is to say, the player with the highest ranking poker hand.

Spread-limit: A betting structure in which a player may choose the amount of the bet between the minimum and maximum. In spread-limit $2-10 7-stud, the opener can choose to bet as little as $2, as much as $10, or any whole dollar amount in between. Raises, however, must at least match the previous bet. If Paul opens with $5, Larry cannot raise by $2 to $7. Larry must raise by at least $5 and as much as $10.

Stack: The amount of money a player has in play. Their table stake.

Starting hand: The cards you hold before the first betting round. In hold 'em, your starting hand is your pocket cards and in 7-stud, your starting hand is your holecards plus your doorcard.

Straight: A poker hand consisting of five cards of consecutive rank. For example, 8-7-6-5-4.

Straight flush: A straight in which the cards are also from the same suit.

Table stakes: A player may only bet or call with money he has on the table at the beginning of the hand. Also, you are not allowed to remove any money from the table until you quit the game entirely.

Tell: A conscious or unconscious act or omission which provides a clue as to the quality of a player's hand.

Texas hold 'em: Usually called just "hold 'em." A form of poker in which each player makes a five card poker hand by combing his two pocket cards with five community cards in the center of the table.

Three of a Kind: A poker hand consisting of three cards of identical rank.

Tight: A game can be tight or a player can be tight. If a player is tight he is playing few hands. If a game is tight, then there are not many players contesting the pot since many of the participants are playing tight. In Canada, a "tight" is a full house.

Tilt: To break from one's usual methods and start to play badly is to "go on tilt."

Trips: Three-of-a-kind.

Two Pair: A poker hand consisting of two cards of one rank and two cards of another rank. For example A-A-9-9 is two pair (often referred to by the higher pair as "aces up").

Under the Gun: The first player to act is said to be "under the gun."

Wheel: Same as a bike. A straight to the five (5-4-3-2-A).

Wild Card: A card which can be used as any other card to make your hand. If jacks are wild then J-7-6-5-4 would be a straight to the eight (the J acts as an eight).

Poker Notes – Improve your game

Poker Notes – **Improve your game**

Poker Notes – **Improve your game**

Poker Notes – Improve your game

Poker Notes – **Improve your game**

Poker Notes – Improve your game

Poker Notes – **Improve your game**

Poker Notes – Improve your game

Poker Notes – **Improve your game**

Poker Notes – **Improve your game**

Poker Notes – **Improve your game**

Poker Notes – **Improve your game**